In Buckeye Country

Photos and Essays
of Ohio Life

Edited by
John Moor and Larry Smith
Introduction by
Scott Russell Sanders

Bottom Dog Press
Literature of the Midwest
c/o Firelands College/ Huron, OH 44839

©1994
Bottom Dog Press
ISBN 0-933087-31-4 / $9.95
All photo images are the copyright property of the individual photographer.
A biographical listing is provided in the back of this book.

CREDITS

Front cover photo is by Charles Cassady Jr.
Buckeye artwork is by Molly Stewart
Cover design by Larry Smith
Typeset in Times Roman by Barbara Wrabel

ACKNOWLEDGMENTS

"The Buckeye" is reprinted from *Grace Notes, Poems* by Rita Dove, by permission of the author and W.W. Norton & Company, Inc. copyright 1989 by Rita Dove.

A segment from Bob Greene's *Be True To Your School* (1988) is reprinted by permission of Macmillan Publishing Company.

William Allen's "Life Itself" is reprinted from his *Walking Distance: An Ohio Odyssey*, (Cincinnati: Black Oak Press, 1993).

Richard Hague's "Basement" first appeared in *Ohio Magazine*, Vol. 12, No. 10, January, 1990.

Larry Smith's "The Company of Widows" first appeared in *The Heartlands Today* 1991.

Robert Fox's "The Farm Not Taken" first appeared in *Confrontation* #52, 1994.

A shorter version of Danny Fulks' "Big Meeting" first appeared as "They Gathered in the Evening" in *Pathway*, Vol. I, No. 3, 1970.

Claude C. Smith's "Hardin County Ditch Watch" first appeared in *Ohio Magazine* Feb. 1993.

Robert Flanagan's "Life's Fiction, Fiction's Life" is reprinted from a longer work in *My Poor Elephant: 27 Male Writers at Work* ed. Eve Shelnutt (Atlanta, Georgia: Longstreet Press, 1992.) An expanded version appeared in *Contemporary Authors Autobiography Series*, Vol. 17, Joyce Nakamura, ed., Gale Research Inc., Detroit, MI.

The Ohio Arts Council helped fund this program with state tax dollars to encourage economic growth, educational excellence and cultural enrichment for all Ohioans.

Table of Contents

THE BUCKEYE

We learned about the state tree
in school—its fruit
so useless, so ugly

no one bothered to
commend the smudged trunk
nor the slim leaves shifting

over our heads. Yet
they were a good thing to kick
along gutters

on the way home,
though they stank like a drunk's piss in the roads.

where the cars had smashed
them. And in autumn
when the spiny helmets split

open,
there was the bald
seed with its wheat-

colored eye.
We loved
the modest countenance beneath
that leathery cap.
We, too, did not want to leave
our mothers.

We piled them up
for ammunition.
We lay down

with them
among the bruised leaves
so that we could

rise, shining.

                    -Rita Dove

Ohio Counties and County Seats

THE BUCKEYES: An Introduction

Years after my father's heart quit, I keep in a wooden box on my desk the two buckeyes that were in his pocket when he died. Once the size of plums, the brown seeds are shriveled now, hollow, hard as pebbles, yet they still gleam from the polish of his hands. He used to reach for them in his overalls or suit pants and click them together, or he would draw them out, cupped in his palm, and twirl them with his blunt carpenter's fingers, all the while humming snatches of old tunes.

"Do you really believe buckeyes keep off arthritis?" I asked him more than once.

He would flex his hands and say, "I do so far."

My father never paid much heed to pain. Near the end, when his worn knee often slipped out of joint, he would pound it back in place with a rubber mallet. If a splinter worked into his flesh beyond the reach of tweezers, he would heat the blade of his knife over a cigarette lighter and slice through the skin. He sought to ward off arthritis not because he feared pain but because he lived through his hands, and he dreaded the swelling of knuckles, the stiffening of fingers. What use would he be if he could no longer hold a hammer or guide a plow? When he was a boy he had known farmers not yet forty years old whose hands had curled into claws, men so crippled up they could not tie their own shoes, could not sign their names.

"I mean to tickle my grandchildren when they come along," he told me, "and I mean to build doll houses and turn spindles for tiny chairs on my lathe."

So he fondled those buckeyes as if they were charms, carrying them with him when our family moved from Ohio at the end of my childhood, bearing them to new homes in Louisiana, then Oklahoma, Ontario, and Mississippi, carrying them still on his final day when pain a thousand times fiercer than arthritis gripped his heart.

The box where I keep the buckeyes also comes from Ohio, made by my father from a walnut plank he bought at a farm auction. I remember the auction, remember the sagging face of the widow whose home was being sold, remember my father telling her he would prize that walnut as if he had watched the tree grow from a sapling on his own land. He did not care for pewter or silver or gold, but he cherished wood. On the rare occasions when my mother coaxed him into a museum, he ignored the paintings or porcelain and studied the exhibit cases, the banisters, the moldings, the parquet floors.

I remember him planing that walnut board, sawing it, sanding it, joining piece to piece to make foot stools, picture frames, jewelry boxes. My own box, a bit larger than a soap dish, lined with red corduroy, was meant to hold earrings and pins, not buckeyes. The top is inlaid with pieces fitted so as to bring out the grain, four diagonal joints converging from the corners toward the center. If I stare long enough at those converging lines, they float free of the box and point to a center deeper than wood.

I learned to recognize buckeyes and beeches, sugar maples and shagbark hickories, wild cherries, walnuts, and dozens of other trees while tramping through the Ohio woods with my father. To his eyes, their shapes, their leaves, their bark, their winter buds were as distinctive as the set of a friend's shoulders. As with friends, he was partial to some, craving their company, so he would go out of his way to visit particular trees, walking in a circle around the splayed roots of a sycamore, laying his hand against the trunk of a white oak, ruffling the feathery green boughs of a cedar.

"Trees breathe," he told me. "Listen."

I listened, and heard the stir of breath.

He was no botanist; the names and uses he taught me were those he had learned from country folks, not from books. Latin never crossed his lips. Only much later would I discover that the tree he called ironwood, its branches like muscular arms, good for axe handles, is known in the books as hophornbeam; what he called tuliptree or canoewood, ideal for log cabins, is officially the yellow poplar; what he called hoop ash, good for barrels and fence posts, appears in books as hackberry.

When he introduced me to the buckeye, he broke off a chunk of the gray bark and held it to my nose. I gagged.

"That's why the old-timers called it stinking buckeye," he told me. "They used it for cradles and feed troughs and peg legs."

"Why for peg legs?" I asked.

"Because it's light and hard to split, so it won't shatter when you're clumping around."

He showed me this tree in late summer, when the fruits had fallen and the ground was littered with prickly brown pods. He picked up one, as fat as a lemon, and peeled away the husk to reveal the shiny seed. He laid it in my palm and closed my fist around it so the seed peeped out from the circle formed by my index finger and thumb. "You see where it got the name?" he asked.

I saw: what gleamed in my hand was the eye of a deer, bright with life. "It's beautiful," I said.

"It's beautiful," my father agreed, "but also poisonous. Nobody eats buckeyes, not even squirrels."

I knew the gaze of deer from living in the Ravenna Arsenal, in Portage County, up in the northeastern corner of Ohio. After supper we often drove the Arsenal's gravel roads, past the munitions bunkers, past acres of rusting tanks and wrecked bombers, into the far fields where we counted deer. One June evening, while mist rose from the ponds, we counted three hundred and eleven, our family record. We found the deer in herds, in bunches, in amorous pairs. We came upon lone bucks, their antlers lifted against the sky like the bare branches of dogwood. If you were quiet, if your hands were empty, if you moved slowly, you could leave the car and steal to within a few paces of a grazing deer, close enough to see the delicate lips, the twitching nostrils, the glossy, fathomless eyes.

The wooden box on my desk holds these grazing deer, as it holds the buckeyes and the walnut plank and the farm auction and the munitions bunkers and the breathing forests and my father's hands. I could lose the box, I could lose the polished seeds, but if I were to lose the memories I would become a bush without roots, and every new breeze would toss me about. All those memories lead back to the northeastern corner of Ohio, the place where I came to consciousness, where I learned to connect feelings with words, where I fell in love with the earth.

It was a troubled love, for much of the land I knew as a child had been ravaged. The ponds in the Arsenal teemed with bluegill and beaver, but they were also laced with TNT from the making of bombs. Because the wolves and coyotes had long since been killed, some of the deer, so plump in the June grass, collapsed on the January snow, whittled by hunger to racks of bones. Outside the Arsenal's high barbed fences, many of the farms had failed, their barns caving in, their topsoil gone. Ravines were choked with swollen couches and junked washing machines and cars. Crossing fields, you had to be careful not to slice your feet on tin cans or shards of glass. Most of the rivers had been dammed, turning fertile valleys into scummy playgrounds for boats.

One free-flowing river, the Mahoning, ran past the small farm near the Arsenal where our family lived during my later years in Ohio. We owned just enough land to pasture three ponies and to grow vegetables for our table, but those few acres opened onto miles of woods and creeks and secret meadows. I walked that land in every season, every weather, following animal trails. But then the

Mahoning, too, was doomed by a government decision, we were forced to sell our land, and a dam began to rise across the river.

If enough people had spoken for the river, we might have saved it. If enough people had believed that our scarred country was worth defending, we might have dug in our heels and fought. Our attachments to the land were all private. We had no shared lore, no literature, no art to root us there, to give us courage, to help us stand our ground. The only maps we had were those issued by the state, showing a maze of numbered lines stretched over emptiness. The Ohio landscape never showed up on postcards or posters, never unfurled like tapestry in films, rarely filled even a paragraph in books. There were no mountains in that place, no waterfalls, no rocky gorges, no vistas. It was a country of low hills, cut over woods, scoured fields, villages that had lost their purpose, roads that had lost their way.

"Let us love the country of here below," Simone Weil urged. "It is real; it offers resistance to love. It is this country that God has given us to love. He has willed that it should be difficult yet possible to love it." Which is the deeper truth about buckeyes, their poison or their beauty? I hold with the beauty; or rather, I am held by the beauty, without forgetting the poison. In my corner of Ohio the gullies were choked with trash, yet cedars flickered up like green flames from cracks in stone; in the evening, bombs exploded at the ammunition dump, yet from the darkness came the mating cries of owls. I was saved from despair by knowing a few men and women who cared enough about the land to clean up trash, who planted walnuts and oaks that would long outlive them, who imagined a world that would have no call for bombs.

How could our hearts be large enough for heaven if they are not large enough for earth? The only country I am certain of is the one here below. The only paradise I know is the one lit by our everyday sun, this land of difficult love, shot through with shadow. The place where we learn this love, if we learn it at all, shimmers behind every new place we inhabit.

A family move carried me away from Ohio thirty years ago; my schooling and marriage and job have kept me away ever since, except for visits in memory and in flesh. I returned to the site of our Portage County farm one cold November day, when the trees were skeletons and the ground shone with the yellow of fallen leaves. From a previous trip I knew that our house had been bulldozed, our yard and pasture had grown up in thickets, and the reservoir had flooded the woods. On my earlier visit I had merely gazed from the car, too numb with loss to climb out. But on this November day, I parked the car, drew on my hat and gloves, opened the door, and walked.

I was looking for some sign that we had lived there, some token of our affection for the place. All that I recognized, aside from the contours of the land, were two weeping willows that my father and I had planted near the road. They had been slips the length of my forearm when we set them out, and now their crowns rose higher than the telephone poles. When I touched them last, their trunks had been smooth and supple, as thin as my wrist, and now they were furrowed and stout. I took off my gloves and laid my hands against the rough bark. Immediately I felt the wince of tears. Without knowing why, I said hello to my father, quietly at first, then louder and louder, as if only shouts could reach him through the bark and miles and years.

Surprised by sobs, I turned from the willows and stumbled away toward the drowned woods, calling to my father. I sensed that he was nearby. Even as I called, I was wary of grief's deceptions. I had never seen his body after he died. By the time I reached the place of his death, a furnace had reduced him to ash. The need to see him, to let go of him, to let go of this land and time, was powerful enough to summon mirages; I knew that. But I also knew, stumbling toward the woods, that my father was here.

At the bottom of a slope where the creek used to run, I came to an expanse of gray stumps and withered grass. It was a bay of the reservoir from which the water had retreated, the level drawn down by engineers or drought. I stood at the edge of this desolate ground, willing it back to life, trying to recall the woods where my father had taught me the names of trees. No green shoots rose. I walked out among the stumps. The grass crackled under my boots, breath rasped in my throat, but otherwise the world was silent.

Then a cry broke overhead and I looked up to see a red-tailed hawk launching out from the top of an oak. I recognized the bird from its band of dark feathers across the creamy breast and the tail splayed like rosy fingers against the sun. It was a red-tailed hawk for sure; and it was also my father. Not a symbol of my father, not a reminder, not a ghost, but the man himself, right there, circling in the air above me. I knew this as clearly as I knew the sun burned in the sky. A calm poured through me. My chest quit heaving. My eyes dried.

Hawk and father wheeled above me, circle upon circle, wings barely moving, head still. My own head was still, looking up, knowing and being known. Time scattered like fog. At length, father and hawk stroked the air with those powerful wings, three beats, then vanished over a ridge.

The voice of my education told me then and tells me now that I did not meet my father, that I merely projected my longing onto a bird. My education may well be right; yet nothing I heard in school, nothing I've read, no lesson reached by logic has ever convinced me as utterly or stirred me as deeply as did that red-tailed hawk. Nothing in my education prepared me to love a piece of the earth, least of all a humble, battered country like northeastern Ohio; I learned from the land itself.

Before leaving the drowned woods, I looked around at the ashen stumps, the wilted grass, and for the first time since moving from this place I was able to let it go. This ground was lost; the flood would reclaim it. But other ground could be saved, must be saved, in every neighborhood, every home place.

For each home ground we need new maps, living maps, stories and poems, photographs and paintings, essays and songs. We need to know where we are, so that we may dwell in our place with a full heart. You are holding now a piece of Ohio's new map. Read *In Buckeye Country*, and the lines may lead you to a center deeper than paper, deeper than words, a firm center where you can make a stand.

Scott Russell Sanders

PREFACE: IN BUCKEYE COUNTRY

I am proud to be a Buckeye even though I reserve most of that pride for two occasions. The first is the annual football game in late November between the Ohio State University and that "team up north." The other is whenever any out-of-stater makes some disparaging remark about Ohio (e.g., "It's so boring.") or one of its cities (i.e., usually Cleveland).

The rest of the time I don't give Ohio or my particular place in Ohio much thought. On most days, I might as well be living in Idaho as in Ohio. For many, familiarity breeds contempt. For me, it seems to breed indifference. Having lived in Ohio all of my 38 years, I was so familiar with the state that I stopped thinking there was anything extraordinary about it some time ago. Like sandpaper, familiarity rubbed and rubbed my point of view about Ohio until all the definition was gone, leaving me with only a smooth, flat outlook on the state.

That is one reason why I welcomed the invitation to co-edit this book. I realized I needed to bring some definition back to my view of Ohio. I wanted to read words and images and ideas and meet people that would once again make Ohio and my relationship to it special. I wanted to see pictures and read essays that would remind me that Ohio isn't boring and that it isn't Idaho. In other words, I was searching for an attitude adjustment.

I found one. Each submission I read worked like a carver's knife etching a distinct design on the smooth, flat surface of my indifference. Slowly, the essays and photographs began to give depth, dimension and meaning to Ohio and Ohioans.

The 22 essays and photographs that were selected for this book give the reader a sense of what makes Ohio unique as seen through the eyes of regional writers and photographers. Granted, while I read many of the essays, I thought to myself, "This could've taken place anywhere." But that is a sign of good writing—the ability to connect with the reader through shared experiences. Ohio serves as the setting for each of these experiences, a regional start with a universal destination.

In the conclusion of his introduction, "The Buckeyes," Scott Russell Sanders talks about the "need" for "new maps, living maps." To the reader he writes, "You are holding now a piece of Ohio's new map." It's an appropriate metaphor for *In Buckeye Country*. The essays and photographs have been organized such that, if they are taken in order, the reader will start at the heart of the state and then move north then circle home in a clockwise direction.

We begin with Stephen Ostrander's "fun" piece that takes us to small towns all over the state to see how they got their names and character. From there, it's on to the Columbus area and the high school days of Bob Greene and a visit with Charlene Fix to the dingy shop of a shoe repairman. We move northward to the Delaware woods where William Allen opens his eyes and heart to Nature. In Cleveland, Amy Sparks reveals the poignant death of a suburban father, and we read the proud endorsements of those who have happily found their places in Ohio — Les Roberts and David Citino.

After a brief stop in the university town of Kent with Diane Fencl, we move into the southeastern part of the state. In Steubenville, we descend with Richard Hague into a basement and then reappear with Larry Smith's panorama of an industrial hometown festival. Family lines are etched in Laura Smith's portrait of her Hungarian grandfather. Phil Boiarski sketches in the hunting grounds and strip mines, Robert Fox what farming life can mean around Athens. Danny Fulks reveals a time of revival meetings; Doug Swift and Gaile Gaitlin are caught in the longing of hills and roads around Cambridge. Near the state's southern point Brian Richards journals a natural life of friends and animals. All are keeping a stewardship of the land.

In Cincinnati Constance Pierce and Kevin Walzer each portray a complex city and their own coming to terms with a place. Joe Napora provides a close and ironic look at the Indian burial mound and nuclear weapons plant near Dayton. The journey ends in Northwest Ohio with a visit to a Harding County ditch with Claude C. Smith and a return to one writer's youth in working class Toledo. Most of these Ohio essayists are writers — novelists, journalists, and poets — all of them finding in Ohio a landscape of the imagination, a place of deep and ambivalent connection from which the writing springs. Like Rita Dove in her opening poem "The Buckeye," they bring together people and places, laying a path for us all to follow.

The journey is comprehensive though arguably incomplete. Its connecting thread tying all of these essays and photographs together is a desire, an enthusiasm, a need to create a sense of place and understand the people who live in that place. *In Buckeye Country* is a celebration of Ohio played out in striking images and words. The book is a reminder of who we are and where we are and why such knowledge is so important. Enjoy.

-John Moor
January 1994

Farmhouse near Columbus ©*Stephen J. Ostrander*

STEPHEN J. OSTRANDER

STEPHEN J. OSTRANDER lives in Grandview Heights, suburban Columbus, where he works at writing field guides to the nature preserves in Ohio and Pennsylvania. He has worked in a variety of forms—writing, photography, wood sculptures—in a variety of jobs—sportswriter, newspaper editor, communications chief, and artist. His work has appeared in many Midwestern publications and in the Sunday magazines of the Cleveland *Plain Dealer*, Columbus *Dispatch*, and Dayton *Daily News*.

As of this publication he claims "two kids, two mortgages, two cars, two cats, but one wife." The author's training in history and nature come across in this "map meditation" on the names that reflect and enrich the Ohio culture. Beneath the "naming" rite of Ohio towns he finds a character that we may be losing to a growing commercialism of town identities.

ON NAMES, PLACES, AND TIME

The latest Ohio highway map, the official one printed by the Department of Transportation, spreads out on the varnished plains of my kitchen table. My finger traces Route 23 south from Columbus to Chillicothe, then southwest an inch. Yes, it is still there—Knockemstiff. I circle it with a pencil. The names runs easterly beneath a circle hardly bigger than a spot which grows on a hair-thin black line designating a paved road barely wide enough for a motorcycle and a sidecar.

And over there, along the Ohio River, is Eureka, and Getaway, and Antiquity. And how about those sharp-edged settlements like Dart, Dent, or Broken Sword; and those frightful sounding places—Hanging Rock, Crooked Tree, or Torch. Can I find those bucolic locations entitled Rainbow, Dawn, Rising Sun, Pearl, Shade or Charm? Yes, they are all still there, those wonderful relics of the frontier, the remnants of Ohio's adolescence and innocence. Their tiny dots on this paper landscape tell me as much about time as about place.

I confess to being a map meditator—someone who studies maps for spiritual guidance, to cure wanderlust, or to learn the lay of the land. Not that I have any place to go, or any purpose in mind. I just look into any map, sometimes for hours. Peter Steinhart is right, "Maps are a way of organizing wonder."

Sometimes I amuse myself by choosing towns from the index and finding them by intersecting the letter and number references. When deeply meditating, I let my eyes wander off the bold-red lines of the interstates (a luxury I cannot afford when driving) to the lesser state roads, and then to the thin fibers marking county and township roads where the asphalt dissolves into dust.

Now in a trance, the "white" on the map, the land, shifts and breathes, and the elastic lines conform to the contour of the land. Just as I once watched clouds make familiar shapes, I trace patterns, figures, faces from the lines that are highways. In this dream, vehicles scurry like ants along the lines; and I recall the photo in my mind of this intersection, filling station to my right where I sometimes refuel and the fast-food restaurant my children enjoy.

Imagine, as I have, that the roads are capillaries, veins, and arteries feeding and depleting a pulsating heart; or that they are the filaments of a spider's web which hold glistening dewdrops; or that they are ropes holding down Gulliver who strains to be freed from his bondage; or that they are the welts of human development, the fleshy symbols of submission. All of this I have seen in my meditations.

Knockemstiff got me started on this meditating business about 10 years ago. Lt. Gov. Myrl Shoemaker was the boss of the Department of Natural Resources. He hailed from Bourneville in Ross County, and being a diligent bureaucrat I searched for its location. That's when Knockemstiff hit me like the proverbial ton of bricks.

Who can resist a place called Knockemstiff? Such a battle cry! The very essence of Whitman's "yawp!" The wolf's lonely howl!

Wait a minute. Surely this must be a backwoods prank, I thought, or some private joke a state cartographer has been pulling for years? (At the time, I had lived in Ohio only four years.) Maybe this is some trap Ohioans spring on newcomers like me. Like westerners have their jackalope ruse, Ohioans have their Knockemstiff gag—something like that. All of them ready to shout the punchline. But, Mr. Shoemaker assured me Knockemstiff was there all right, in his legislative district.

The name kept tugging on me. Finally, on one scorching summer day I headed for the wilds of Ross County.

Upon reaching Chillicothe, I traveled southwest on Route 50, turned south on the Blain Highway (an exaggerated rating for this pocked pavement), then right on a road charmingly called Kidnocker Lane. A fast right put me on Black Run Road. This led to Knockemstiff, a mile away, and eventually to another town known as Storms.

Knockemstiff clings to the banks of Black Run, a tributary of Paint Creek, not exactly the most inviting names for streams. The slender utility poles which carry electricity barely stand higher than fenceposts. In the yards of homes on Black Run Road, chickens and dogs roam chaotically among the miscellany of crippled Chevys and farm implements. Porches sag under the weight of broken appliances and crates. Laundry dances in the breeze.

Don't look for destination signs. You will know you are *there* when you see the "Knockemstiff USA" sign on the side of Happy's Bar, the sign a courtesy of the Coca-Cola company.

Happy's Bar was a white-washed blockhouse stuck in gray mud. The pickup trucks outside were parked where they had coughed to a stop, the driver's door of one of them was left open. These vehicles of burden, their headlights facing in different directions, seemed to graze on the few patches of grass.

Conversation ceased when I entered the tavern. Bar stools creaked, and all I saw were shadows until my eyes could focus in the dusky light. When I reached the bar a fellow wearing a Budweiser cap spit a mouthful of tobacco juice into a Dixie cup. I was not sure if he had cleared his mouth in order to speak, or to fight. (One does not want to inadvertently swallow a wad of Red Man while throwing a sucker punch, does one?)

Just so I was not mistaken as a cop, card shark, repo man, or some other undesirable, I told the bartender my name, hometown, profession, and...

"You'll be wanting to know how this place got its name," said the bartender, a husky-voiced woman in her late forties. She was rinsing her dog's bowl. The dog, a dusty setter of some kind, snored beneath a nearby table.

"Why, yes," I responded. "You see, I've been wondering..."

"Cuz we knock 'em stiff," explained the tobacco spitter, staring absently at the pool players in the back of the bar, not at me.

"You'll see, if you come back here around 11 p.m. tonight," cackled the tavern owner.

"Or sooner," snapped the tobacco-spitter, his pale glassy-eyed face now glared hard at me, and his mechanic's hand throttled on the neck of a Rolling Rock.

After a few tense seconds, a grin undermined his threat. Then we both laughed—him because he had spooked another nosy stranger, and me at the relief of not being knocked stiff.

"Listen up, pal. You're not going to die today," the tobacco-spitter assured me. So, over a round of Rolling Rocks, my treat, I got the story on the founding of Knockemstiff.

One day long ago two men (nobody remembers their names) commenced a rib-kicking, ball-busting, call-the-cops brawl. The cause of the commotion varies among storytellers, but many figure it had something to do with a woman, or whiskey, or money, or all three. In those rough-and-ready days, the winning pugilist, having earned the affection of the crowd, got the town named after him. But this particular melee ended in a draw. Both combatants knocked each other stiff.

Even into the late 1970s Knockemstiff lived up to its name. Young studs from nearby towns often sowed their oats in Happy's by re-enacting the battle of the town's founding fathers. Once a couple of patrons stole an episode from a TV western and rode horses right into the bar. It got so bad that folks thought the sheriff had set up a substation in the parking lot.

Fearing that the town was backsliding, some thoughtful villager lobbied for a new name—Shady Glen. Somehow that prompted the "stiffs" at Happy's to clean up their act. When the Shady Glen idea disappeared, so had much of the riff-raff.

"Now we're down to just three or four fights a month and the horses have to park outside," the tavern keeper concluded.

Back home, meditating again, I discovered other towns with wild and compelling names. They carry me back to the time when Ohio still had room for town building. The names tell me how the land treated my ancestors, and how they treated it back. Their optimism, humor, vision, and hardships speak out in these names.

My favorite names explode like firecrackers in the middle of a wilderness night. Some testify to a struggle on the frontier. They are honest and spontaneous names, often reflecting the character of both the land and its rugged individuals. The stories behind them give all of us a sense of belonging to a place faraway and a time long ago.

Like Knockemstiff, one Trumbull County settlement started with a black eye. In 1840 a temperance preacher ranting against "likker" declared this nameless crossroads hamlet "a perfect Sodom." An unrepentant villager shot back, "then that's what we'll call this Godforsaken place." Today, the place is known as Sodom Corners. Teetotalers in Belmont County later avenged the parson by naming their colony Temperanceville.

The jokers who named the Ohio River town of Fly thought they had found the shortest and most revolting name. But they were outdone by a community in Fulton County calling itself Ai, meaning "heap of ruin." In Biblical times a Christian army sacked the city of Ai because of its licentiousness and intemperance.

Many settlements eventually scraped the mud off of their boots. Places like Cabintown, Plasterbed, Tally Ho, Snaketown, Scant, Grogtown, Dogtown, Cyclone, Squeal, Straight Out, Toadtown, and Buzzard's Glory gave way to Dayton, Marblehead, McCuneville, Florida, West Union, Pickereltown, Plano, Wayland, Ankeneytown, East Danville, Museville, and New Vienna.

Naming towns has been serious business to folks who had prosperity on their minds. Playing it safe, these pilgrims borrowed the names of famous locations on the globe (Toledo and Athens come to mind); or of Founding Fathers (Washington Court House, Madison, Franklin, etc.); or they commemorated the American Revolution with Independence, Constitution, Congress, Bunker Hill, or Patriot. These founders hoped that some of the fame of their namesakes would rub off in the Ohio country.

Some emigrants thought a proper East Coast name would tame the Ohio country. The Virginians who bedded down in the military tract between the Scioto and Miami rivers must have thought they could recreate their beloved Tidewater with names like Williamsburg, Staunton, Lynchburg, and Fairfax. And what about those damn Yankees declaring their colonies Hartford, Greenwich, Avon, Norwalk, etc. after parking in the Western Reserve of Northeastern Ohio. Did they still think they lived in Connecticut?

And then there were the unabashed optimists whose town names—Empire, Atlas, Triumph, Mecca, Hope, Delightful, Continental, Mt. Healthy, Joy, Provident—made even the most enthusiastic Chamber of Commerce types shrink.

Sometimes "naming" got exasperating. Pioneers at a meeting in a Washington County community could not settle on any of six selections. Finally, somebody broke the stalemate and shouted, "It will be a relief to get this thing settled, and a relief not to have to cross the river to a post office, so let's call it Relief." The townspeople approved.

Another time, the settlers of a fledgling Preble County village tossed around names into the wee morning hours. A weary farmer suggested they call the place after the first thing they see in the morning. Being early risers, they watched the sunrise; hence, Morning Sun. Ohio's golden mornings also impressed the natives of Rising Sun, Aurora, Golden Corners, and Dawn.

In 1897, when the gold rush peaked in Alaska's Klondike region, Guernsey County miners struck a fat vein of coal. They called the town that grew up around the depository, Klondyke. But that worried folks who predicted the name would convert the settlement into a disorderly gold rush camp. After a debate, the residents compromised on Kipling, after the British author Rudyard Kipling.

Ohio has its share of burgs named after Indians (Wapakoneta, Chillicothe, etc.); and wildlife (Eagleville, Cygnet, Beaver, etc.); and trees (White Oak, Sycamore, Lindentree, etc.); and places "fair" (Fairfield, Fairview, Fairport, etc.); and pleasant (Pleasantville, Pleasant Bends, Pleasant Grove, etc.); and its "corners," like Toot's Corners, one of 22 corners in Mahoning County.

We have company towns too. Phoneton (Miami County) started as a colony founded by the Bell Telephone Company in 1893 for the employees of its local works. The Trumbull Phalanx Company, a consortium of cooperative mills run by socialists in the 1840's, influenced the naming of Phalanx. Places called Excello, Brilliant, Red Lion, Magnolia, and Montra owe their names to factories there.

Towns stuck between two other places equidistant apart got "middle" for a prefix. Diminutive Midway, in Madison County, supposedly lies halfway between Philadelphia and Chicago, while Middletown is the same distance from Cincinnati and Dayton.

Numbers sufficed for some locations. Seven Mile in Butler County is 7 miles away from Fairfield and Middletown. Seventeen in Tuscarawas County grew around Lock 17 on the Ohio Canal. The villages of Sixteen Mile Stand and Twenty Mile Stand mark distances from Cincinnati on an old stagecoach route. And don't count out Five Mile and Upper Five Mile in Brown County.

One town name has undergone an evolution (my apologies to Darwin in Meigs County). Fee Town (after founder William Fee), became Feetown, then Feel City, Feelicity, and finally Felicity (Clermont County).

Guessing the origin of town names can be risky. The law abiding folks in Crooksville quickly point out their town is named after its first postmaster, Joseph E. Crooks, and not for crooks, cutthroats, or con men who lived there.

Modern day Newcomerstown heartily welcomes "newcomers," but in frontier days the name reminded inhabitants to be wary of outsiders. The name comes from the legend of Chief Eagle Feather who enraged his wife Mary Harris (a white woman abducted by Indians as a child) when he brought home another wife, an Indian woman. War erupted in the household and Eagle Feather was murdered. Mary Harris accused the "newcomer" of the dirty deed. The Indians caught the suspect fleeing down the Tuscarawas River.

The source of Blue Ball in Butler County is misunderstood. College fraternity pledges posing for photographs beside the village sign think the name stems from a painful condition afflicting male genitalia. It doesn't, of course. Weary stagecoach travelers asked the driver to stop at the inn that hung a blue ball outside its door. (Many travelers were illiterate, so innkeepers hung ornaments or signs depicting animals or symbols to be remembered.) The popular stop supplanted the original name of the town, Gifford.

Clarence Reminder did such a great job as mayor of a Summit County community that folks named the village after him. In doing so, however, they wiped out all reminders of the place's name before Reminder got elected.

Healthy people thrive in Jumbo (Hardin County), but they are not giants. The hamlet memorializes Jumbo the Elephant, a performer in P.T. Barnum's circus. The popular pachyderm was killed in a train wreck.

Don't hunt for vineyards nor chronic complainers in Winesburg. This Holmes County village owes its name (with an American twist that caught novelist Sherwood Anderson's ear) to Weinsburg, Germany.

Abandon thoughts that Coolville in Athens County derived its name from cold weather, or because its inhabitants are aloof, or perennially "hip." The name has been traced to a pioneer named Simeon Cooley. Gore in Hocking County does not remember a massacre, but stems from a dressmaker's term.

Though it has had its share of winners, Champion in Trumbull County recognizes its founder Henry Champion, who is not linked to a popular brand of spark plug (made in Toledo). Likewise, places like Dull, Hawk, Overpeck, Mt. Joy, Jobtown, Stoutsville all pay tribute to early settlers, not to any peculiar traits of the residents nor the prospects of the town.

Ohio's pioneers never forgot a kindness. A century and a half ago, David Bennett tapped a beer for customers in his new grocery in Clark County. He told everybody toting a mug to "pitch in." Customers appreciated the hospitality and named the place Pitchin. Quakers in Preble County called their village Gratis to honor the county commissioners who gave them township status for "gratis."

By accident, Utopia has become exactly what it was supposed to be. The town proves you cannot plan for perfection, it just happens. In 1844 some Fourierites hoping to build a perfect society established a colony on the banks of the Ohio River in Clermont County. Within two years, though, their noble cause had failed. Spiritualists took over the place, but their dream of a manufacturing center was wiped out by a flood in 1847. Taking the hint, the survivors gave up the notion of creating a paradise at the place.

Today, Utopia meets the expectation of a handful of residents. Nobody here feels unfulfilled because it lacks a gourmet restaurant, or a shopping mall. There's enough space between neighbors to keep them neighborly, and plenty of peace and quiet, what some people mistake as boredom. And when life in Utopia gets too vagarious, there's always the Ohio River to look at, its current an endless source of monotonous meditation.

Tranquility also is a self-fulfilling settlement. Indeed, it has been tranquil there ever since John T. Wilson opened his general store. During a trip to Cincinnati, a wholesaler asked Wilson where to deliver the goods. The Adams County merchant pointed to a place on a map. "Right there, where there is tranquility."

You just won't hear contemporary builders knocking around names like Knockemstiff. Nobody has a sense of humor about these things anymore. The frontier, the source of such names and humor, long ago disappeared. In fact, looking at the map, Ohio is fully occupied, too grown up, I guess, for town names inspired by broken limbs.

Imagine a realtor trying to sell homes in new developments called "Get Bent" or "Rat's Nest" or "Wannabe Heights"? No way. Too much money at stake. Cannot risk offending buyers.

And names like Utopia, Tranquility, Aurora, Mecca are goners, unless you are appealing to New Agers who cannot afford Sausalito or Santa Fe. Forget town names with numbers in them too. Face it, kids from places called "High Five" or "Seven Up" would be knocked stiff from Cleves to Conneaut.

So, what goes into a name nowadays? When suburbs arrived so too came those innocuous, comfy-sounding names. You know the ones I mean. They end in "heights," or "hills," or "park," or "manor," or "view." They announce orderly, educated, well-mannered, pastoral places, havens from the uncertainties and rigors of living in the city or the country.

Now consider the latest fortifications, those carefully laid out and manicured residential subdivisions (dare I call them anti-places?) within suburbs. Their names—That-shire Place or What-chester Winds, or Hidden This or Overthere Bay—come right out of a desktop at an ad agency, part of a marketing plan. Nothing honest stamped on these names. No rugged individualism detected. No "place" really described.

So, back to my maps. And there is Revenge, Bobo, Sharpeye, Deserted Camp, Bulkhead, Moonville, Uno, and Honesty. Ah yes, and Gem, Best, Windfall, Paradise, Celeryville, Kitchen, Purity, Reform, Veto. And don't forget Welcome, Pulse, Friendship, Outville, Vulcan, Angel, and Stovetown. Over there, Convoy, Magnetic Springs, Modest, Science Hill, Peerless Station, Zens City, Keno, Tinny, Tick Ridge, Tunnel. Cannot forget Saltpetre, Gravel Bank, Cow Run, Flat Iron, Moons, Postboy, Rock, Maximo, Pink and Ink (names to delight Dr. Seuss methinks), Booktown. Don't skip over Wortsville, Santoy, Joetown, Ironspot, Climax, Happy Corners, Bloomer, Acme, Zone, Moats, Spore. And Pansy, Big Onion, Child, Wegee, Widowville, Comet, Sulphur, Lick, Slabtown...

Union Station Arch, Columbus ©*Becky Linhardt*

BOB GREENE

BOB GREENE is an Ohioan whose syndicated column for the Chicago *Tribune* appears in more than 200 newspapers in the United States. He is also a contributing editor to *Esquire* magazine, where his "American Beat" column appears each month. He is contributing correspondent for "ABC News Nightline." His eight previous books include the national best-seller *Good Morning, Merry Sunshine* (1985), *Be True To Your School* (1988), *American Beat* (1984), *Hang Time* with Michael Jordan (1985), and *Our Children's Children* with D.G. Fulford (1993).

The year is 1964, and the place is a suburb of Columbus, Ohio. Bob Greene is a high school junior who is keeping a diary for one year. In this selection, Greene exposes us to several significant slices from his daily life, from a New Year's Eve kiss to the wearing of his letter jacket in a downtown Columbus store. Using a journal form, Greene captures an era.

From *BE TRUE TO YOUR SCHOOL*

January 1

Right at midnight last night, just as I was kissing Candy Grossman, something popped into my mind.

It was this: I wonder if a new year is really supposed to feel brand new?

We were at Allen Schulman's parents' apartment; his folks were out for New Year's Eve, and they let us have the place. Allen is the only one of us who doesn't live in a house; his parents have the penthouse in the only "luxury high-rise apartment building" in Columbus, and we were all dancing to "Be True to Your School" and looking out the windows toward downtown. Columbus really looks different from seventeen stories in the air.

The dancing had me feeling good. We had been doing the Skip all night, and that makes you get all out of breath; Pongi had a date with Lindsey Alexander, and he was showing off, doing the Pony, but the rest of us were just skipping back and forth like we learned from "Dance-O-Rama" on Channel 4.

We turned off the record player and turned the radio on to WCOL, and Bob Harrington, the disc jockey, counted down the seconds until midnight. Then we all kissed our dates; I guess that's what you're supposed to do at midnight on New Year's Eve, but I felt sort of silly, like I was trying to be a grown-up at one of my parents' parties, instead of being sixteen years old, which is what I am. I had never kissed Candy before—we don't even know each other all that well, she's just a friend of my younger sister Debby—but because it was midnight we had to pretend that this was old stuff to us.

So I kissed Candy and I was thinking about what the new year is going to be like. I half expected, in those seconds just after midnight, to feel like everything had changed and that I was starting all over again. But I didn't feel that way, of course; I opened my eyes and I was still in Allen's parents' apartment, and everybody was still kissing their dates.

I thought about going off to find a telephone to call Lindy's number and see if she was home, but that would have been rude to Candy, and I don't know what I would have said, anyway.

I just hope that 1964 is better than 1963.

January 2

It was snowing this morning when I woke up. The clock radio next to my bed went off, and I was hoping that the voices would say that the schools were all closed because of the weather. But they didn't; the news came on a five till seven and there was nothing at all about school closings, and then the music came back. "Louie, Louie" is number one in Columbus this week.

The reason that I was hoping for no school is that we were supposed to have a test in Schacht's Algebra class this morning, and I didn't study at all over Christmas vacation. Mr. Schacht is the hardest teacher in the school, and there was no way that I was going to pass the test. The rumor around school is that he was written up in *Life* magazine about fifteen years ago for being one of the best teachers in America; they were supposed to have printed an "honor roll' of the country's finest educators, and Schacht was supposed to have made it, with a picture and everything. The only teacher from Bexley High School on the list. He was standing by the blackboard in his brown suit when we came into class—he had chalk all over the sleeves, as usual. He was smiling, and he asked us if we'd had a good vacation. We all sort of mumbled, and then he said he had a surprise for us—he was postponing the test. So the disaster will be delayed.

In the study hall next period Carol Lowenthal sat next to me; she's one of the very best-looking of the sophomore girls. She said that she heard that Chuck Shenk and I are great dancers; she said, "Next year is really going to be terrific."

Well, first of all I'm not that good a dancer at all. And second of all, I knew what she was getting at. She and her friends—Linda McClure and all the rest of them—are already thinking ahead to next year, when all of the seniors have gone off to college and all of us juniors become the oldest guys in the school. Notice that she didn't say anything about going out with Chuck or me this year; it's next year she has in mind.

Oh, well. It was nice to hear that she was interested, anyway.

After school we had paste-up for our pages in the *Torch* office. I was pasting up page 1—that's the page I'm editor of—and Judy Furman came over and said, "So, did you go out with Lindy New Year's Eve?"

I just looked at her.

I'm listening to "Hootenanny" on WBNS right now. Mom and Dad are in their room watching television; Debby is doing her homework and Timmy's on the phone with one of his friends. I think WBNS realizes that because it refuses to play any rock and roll, it's losing all of its younger listeners to WCOL. WBNS seems to figure that by having "Hootenanny" on the air every night it can get some of us back.

I don't know—I really like folk music, but it gets pretty boring after an hour or so.

TV Guide says that James Dean is on Channel 10 in "East of Eden" at eleven-thirty. If I pull my portable TV close to the bed so the light from the screen doesn't show under the bottom of my bedroom door, and if I keep the sound low enough, Mom and Dad won't know that I've got it on so late. I think I'll stay up and watch.

January 3

French quiz this afternoon. I may have flunked it.

Tonight there was a basketball game against Whitehall. All of us (ABCDJ) went to it together.

ABCDJ is what the five of us call each other. We've been best friends all during high school, and I would bet that we remain best friends for the rest of our lives. The letters stand for the first initials of each of our first names.

A is Al Schulman. His parents' apartment is where the New Year's Eve party was. Besides being the only one of us who doesn't live in a house, Allen is the only one of us who doesn't go to Bexley. He goes to military school down in West Virginia, which is a drag—he's only home for Christmas these last couple of weeks, but in a few days he's going back to his school. I like him as well as anybody in the world, but it's tough having one of your best friends not even be around more than half of the time. It's great when he's here, though—when ABCDJ walked into the school gym tonight, we really felt complete.

B, of course, is me.

C is Chuck Shenk. His father is a big-deal businessman, but the thing I like the most about Chuck is that he doesn't seem to care about anything. You could tell him that the world was going to end at midnight, and he'd probably just toss his head to one side and then say, "Let's go to the Toddle House for cheeseburgers and banana cream pie." A lot of the big athletes in the school don't particularly like Chuck, but I think that's because they don't really understand him. I think he has that problem a lot—my dad, for example, doesn't particularly get along with him, either. People think he's being a wiseass because he's always grinning at what they say, and not saying anything in return. I don't think he's trying to be wise; I just don't think he wastes a lot of time thinking about things one way or the other.

D is Danny Dick. Dan's one of the best tennis players in the state of Ohio— he was one of only three or four guys in our class, in any sport, to letter our freshman year. Sometimes he seems to be living in a world of his own—he talks about an imaginary frog named Reedeep Reeves—but watch him on that tennis court and you've never seen anything like it in your life. Some people rag him because he's short; I think they're just jealous because as big as they are, Dan was the one who was wearing a Bexley letter jacket way before they were. He'll get his revenge soon enough; his older brother Dicky Dick is a real big guy, and Dicky grew late, too, so Dan will be catching up. The Dick family has a great-looking gray '56 Thunderbird convertible, which Dan gets to drive all he wants. There's only room for one other person in it, so we can never take it out when we all want to cruise together, but boy, is it beautiful.

J is for Jack Roth. He's my oldest friend in the world—we became best friends when we were five years old in kindergarten, which was eleven years ago. His house on Ardmore has a little hill on the street side of the backyard, and when we were kids we used to play Audie Murphy and charge up the hill with toy guns. In a way, Jack seems like the oldest of all of us, even though we're all the same age. His mom died last year, and he's the only one of us who doesn't have both parents alive. It's funny—Jack and I have always been able to talk about just about anything, but we've never talked about that. I've noticed it, though—Jack just seems older now, and I think that's what did it.

So anyway, ABCDJ were all in the stands at the game tonight. We went out into the lobby at half time to get popcorn, and who do we bump into but Lindy and her friends. I immediately felt myself going into a daze; she said something that I couldn't hear, and Allen just walked up to her and told her to go away. That's why I think I like him so much; he knew that if it were up to me I'd stand there and try to talk to her and end up not being cool at all, so he was cool for me.

January 4

Today's Saturday; at noon Dave Frash and Tim Greiner and I went downtown to the Lazarus department store, and I bought a guitar. It has steel strings and it cost nineteen dollars.

I sat there in the musical instrument department of Lazarus and tried to play it; I have no idea how to play, but Dave already has one, and he said you could learn it pretty easily from a book. So I bought an instruction book; the front half shows you how to make the chords, and the back half has songs that you can play.

Dave and Tim aren't part of ABCDJ; Dave is the quarterback on the football team and Tim is the catcher on the baseball team, so they run with a different crowd—the big athletes. It's funny; I run with my friends and it's a pretty self-contained group. They run with their friends, the star football and basketball and baseball players, and that's a pretty self-contained group, too. They only place that we overlap is with each other—it's like we're each others' only contact with two different parts of the Bexley universe. We sit together whenever we can in classes and pass notes back and forth, and let each other know what's going on with our different groups.

Dave has an idea—if we can all get good enough on our guitars, we'll get a hootenanny group up for the school talent show in the spring. The idea is, we'd be like the Bexley version of the New Christy Minstrels or the Kingston Trio.

We wore our letter jackets downtown. I always like that; when you're walking through Lazarus you see all the guys from the other schools around town—North, East, Arlington, Worthington—and you kind of check them out from the corner of your eye. Our jackets are dark blue, with a white "B" on the front. I lettered in tennis last year, when I was a sophomore; I'm the first to admit that, in the Bexley hierarchy, tennis doesn't rank nearly as high as football or basketball or baseball, but a letter's a letter. You're not supposed to show any emotion about things like that, but the day I got my letter was probably the best day of my life...

Girl admires largest Slippery Elm
at Sugar Grove, Ohio ©Stephen J. Ostrander

WILLIAM ALLEN

WILLIAM ALLEN lives in rural Delaware County, Ohio and teaches creative writing at Ohio State University. He is the author of the novel *To Tojo from Billy-Bob Jones* and three acclaimed books of creative nonfiction: *The Fire in the Birdbath and Other Disturbances* (1986), *Starkweather*, and *Walking Distance: An Ohio Odyssey* (Black Oak Books, 1993), from which this essay is derived.

In "Life Itself" Allen takes us on a small track through a nearby woods that lead to a universal awareness. In the animal life that surrounds him he finds wonder. His own humor and intelligence soothe us, even as they awaken our deeper consciousness.

LIFE ITSELF

Nature had hardly existed for me in Delaware County on Winter Road before that spring. Much of the lack of nature, of course, had to do with my being unaware of it, but on my own property it also had to do with my domesticated cats.

The year before Eddie and the family moved in, I had taken in a pregnant cat during the winter. It wasn't altruism. I hated that diarrhea-ridden beast, but she had attractive calico fur, and I wanted her kittens. She had four in my basement. Two I kept. The other two I personally took to Laura and Lisa's home in Corpus Christi in an approved pet carrier on a commercial airline. They named them Taffy and Misty and played with them and fed them. But Eddie had decided that the cats must live exclusively outside. As city cats sometimes will under such conditions, they finally went feral. Their fur became unkempt and they would flee in terror at anyone's approach. Eddie caught a final glimpse of Misty at the kitchen window one night, and that was the end of them.

By contrast, their sisters on Winter Road thrived. They especially thrived on chipmunks and young squirrels. I tried to save what I could, but it was hard. The creatures would bite me, for one thing. Then the chipmunks kept going into shock, weaving and lurching in confusion, often wandering into the gaping jaws of my pets as I held them at bay. The point is, I had put these basically domesticated animals in the country, and in a small way had thrown off the natural balance of the animal population. It wasn't entirely unlike when man first took his dogs and cats and rats with him to parts of the New World and drove many local species to extinction. I think my cats murdered over a hundred chipmunks in one year. It was a form of recreation for them. They were nothing like the skinny, ragged-looking homeless cats that came skulking by searching for a meal and a place to stay the night. My fat cats would kill with their fur still fluffed. Because of them, the only wildlife that would come close were skunks and killer raccoons and other dominant creatures which created their own problems.

But within a month of my friend Eddie's arrival, I was pet-free. The cats were gone, and their wildlife prey soon crept and crawled and charged over the ridgeline and right up to the house. Of course, I'm not blaming Eddie for what happened to poor Esme and her brutish sister, Big Dog, but I will say he tried to take advantage of the situation.

Esme, the smart one, had taken to roaming. Sometimes she would be gone for days. Finally after one of those absences, I found her in the back of the garage. She was stiff with one eye open. She had apparently died happy, though, licking an empty plastic taco sauce bag. Her tail stuck out like a bottle brush.

Big Dog sniffed the corpse and ran off down the road. Later, I noticed her squashed remains on a nearby bridge crossing the Olentangy.

Eddie tried to stop me from giving Esme a decent burial. He wanted her for purposes of dissection. Then he planned to boil her down for her skeleton. I'm not a sentimentalist, but I was repulsed and refused.

The incident jogged my memory of the old days, when dissecting cats was part of Eddie's college studies. No matter what a cat is like in life, preserved in death they all have much in common. Their mouths are wide open, with the tongue lolling out at an unnatural angle. The roof of each cat's mouth is crossed by ridges, quite visible even from a distance. The whiskers, or *vibrissae* as Eddie called them, glisten and somehow seem longer than they ought to be. Perhaps most appalling of all are the eyes, which are open and to me seem to retain in some unfathomable way the cat's final vision of the world, as well as its last plea for mercy.

This wasn't going to happen to my poor Esme, even though in her grisly death she let life return to Winter Road. Nine-year-old Laura watched quietly as I buried my pet down near Snake Lake. Then, as spring advanced, there came the Great Delaware Animal Invasion of 1986.

Until then, life beyond the ridgeline had been a mystery that I heard rather than saw—great shrieks, moans, yaps, howls, hisses, thrashing and splashing sounds that were startling and unnerving. For instance, I was sitting out one night and heard, I was convinced, a night stalker—a human hunter, or a murderer, I thought—stepping on limbs and snapping them. I crept over toward the ridge, then heard a loud slapping splash on the water, which sent me and probably a hundred frogs diving for cover. It wasn't a person at all, but a beaver sounding his warning when he heard me. The next day I found the beginning of his new dam—limbs neatly cut and placed at right angles to one another exactly at the point where Snake Lake turns into a stream.

Also, the autumn before, I had seen migrating blue herons with their enormous wing spans and S-shaped necks and long beaks gliding down over the ridgeline into Snake Lake in ever-tightening spirals, as well as flocks of pintails who kamikazied in, the males leading with authoritative whistles, the females bringing up the rear, quacking. Occasionally, on the very edge of the ridge, indistinct beasts would appear. Usually I would hear them, briefly see their red eyes and vague shapes, then they would be gone.

Young Laura and I were out on the observation deck with the telescope one evening, doing some casual observing, when from behind two fir trees between the house and the ridgeline, we heard sounds echoing as though from an earlier time on earth. The sounds were so loud and primitive and violent that I thought that a kill must be taking place behind those trees. Then, in a fast but easy lope, a fox appeared and ran along the ridge in the direction of the river. It was a red fox, I learned, because of the white tip on its tail. Then its adversary, an opossum, appeared for a moment before it lumbered over the edge into the darkness. As terrifying as the brief fight had sounded, I don't think that either animal was especially hurt.

Red and gray squirrels, more than I had seen before, began romping high in the oaks and beeches near the house. They seemed to compete for limb space, raising their tails high and twitching them at one another. They were fearless up there as they leapt from one tree to another, and I assumed they never fell. But I was wrong: One day Laura watched a squirrel venture out on the tip of a dead limb at least a hundred feet high, when the limb snapped. It's a terrible sight to see something alive fall that far.

Laura screamed and covered her eyes. I wanted to shut my eyes, too, but I also wanted to watch it hit, to see just exactly what would happen. Would it be a kind of living bomb, the way people are when their parachutes don't open? The squirrel took a long time to reach the ground—too long, it seemed. I looked closely and saw that it was sort of gliding down, balancing, using skin stretched between its legs and body to catch the air—and this wasn't a flying squirrel, either. When it did hit, it bounced, sat as though dazed for a few moments, and then went back up the tree, seeming fine. Since Laura missed it all, I had a hard time convincing her the squirrel was all right. She was determined to feed all the squirrels peanuts after that so they could stay on the ground, and we tried, but by-and-large they were confused by the unseasonal nuts and buried them.

Literally hundreds of chipmunks appeared after the cats were gone, to my relief, since I thought they had all been killed. New holes of many different sizes began to appear in the ground around the house, and I had no idea what might be living in all of them.

At first, nature's invasion didn't trouble me at all. Laura and I enjoyed meeting these new creatures. But when I realized that some groundhogs had taken up residence beneath the observation deck, I began to grow concerned. I was trying to watch the sky through my telescope and think about such things as cycling comets bombarding our primitive oceans with organic molecules, perhaps giving start to life and the evolution of man. But the groundhogs, unconcerned with cycles and the continuation of life, just recognized a likely spot for a new home. I had put a lot of time and effort into this strong, reinforced part of my larger deck, considering that at the time I hadn't been as serious an astronomer as I became after the comet. Now when I wanted to use my telescope, I didn't want to have unsettling noises or movement beneath my feet.

I had heard how groundhogs can burrow through anything, even foundations, and, beyond that, my particular groundhogs had started grinding down their incisors on the underside of my expensive, weather-treated wood decking. It helped them keep those teeth from growing back up into their jaws and through their brainpans.

Were they actually using one of my window wells, now covered by decking, as the start of a burrow? If they were, I was in trouble because all the main plumbing for the house was next to one of the wells, and a good bite through a copper pipe could ruin me. As the groundhogs came and went over the weeks, I wondered if they were planning to hibernate down here. If they were, I was really in trouble because they sleep so soundly, I had heard, that they expend almost no energy and come out in the spring almost as fat as when they went in.

And the groundhogs were just the early settlers. Now such creatures as skunks and raccoons seemed to be taking interest in the spot just under where I stood gazing at the stars. Groundhogs apparently are nature's landlords, only they don't charge rent. They won't even defend their territory, and just leave a burrow if a potential tenant wants it.

I couldn't see very well under the deck, or crawl in, and it occurred to me that Laura was the only one small enough to go find out what was taking place. But would she? No, she said, except perhaps for money, and a lot of it, too. Since Eddie was usually a skinflint, only loose with a dollar during rare bouts of hedonomania, I seemed generous by comparison and Laura had concluded that I was rich. She might have had a transcendent nature, but she still was of this world, and much of her energy was devoted to getting my cash. So in the matter of the deck, I refused on principle, for the time being, but I knew that if any serious nesting started under there I eventually might have to cough it up.

As it turned out, hibernation and nesting had already been going on since late the preceding autumn. I discovered this when a six-month-old groundhog climbed or fell into one of my window wells and couldn't get out. My wells are the kind that look like halves of galvanized washtubs buried up against the foundation of the house, with a little window down in there to let light into the basement. They help make basements nicer to be in, but are useless if you build a deck over them, as I had done.

When the little hog went in, I couldn't get at him from the outside, so I went down in the basement and looked at him from close range, as if he were in an aquarium. He was frantically clawing, first at the big tub around him, then at the glass; he obviously felt that he was in trouble.

That part of the basement was dark and full of cobwebs. The window was hard to get to. I wasn't sure if it was corroded shut or not, or, if I did get it open, what the hog would do. I got a chair and sat down to think all this through, keeping a curious eye on the little creature. He reminded me of a drowning rat.

For me just to sit in a chair and think at a time like this seemed odd to Laura, who was standing behind me and wanting something done fast, partly because of the hideous, primeval shrieking that had started. But the only way for me to solve a problem is to contemplate it. I don't automatically jump into dynamic action like a lot of people. In this case, even in the dim light, I could see that the hog was mostly made of teeth—great beaver-like teeth, and I had enough sense to know that I had to be careful here.

Finally, I checked the window, which in fact was rusted shut, but I saw some sort of slotted metal strips holding the glass to the frame, and I found that they could be removed. It was when I was jiggling one of the clips that the hog first saw me, and his reaction was discouraging. He backed up against the tub and pressed down into the dirt until almost all that was left were his teeth. They were clicking together in the oddest way.

Laura agreed to help me trap the hog in a box with a screen on top so he could breathe and see, and also so we could see him. If we managed that without him biting me or—my worst fear—escaping into the dark recesses of the basement, then I would decide what to do with him.

I put on gloves and got the glass out which afforded him an escape route, but the hog's instincts drove him the other way, into the dirt beneath the window well. An older hog might have escaped that way since groundhogs are wonderful diggers, but this one wouldn't turn his back on me in order to dig. Still, he got most of his body out of sight somehow, except for his teeth. As I reached for him, even more primeval-sounding hisses and growls and yowling moans came out of what seemed to be an ever-growing yaw.

I grabbed for the head, but not very determinedly, and he bit the end of the finger of my glove. These were thick, leather gloves, and his incisors didn't hurt much, so I just let him bite. It was the best thing I could have done because it made the hog feel inadequate. "This isn't working," he thought, or I believe that's what he thought. Since I don't know how groundhogs think, but do believe in interpretation of action, I like to guess at their thought processes. Some scientists abhor this, but others don't seem to mind.

I let the hog chew until he stopped, then tried in earnest to grab him, but his little rat-sized body was hard to get at. Touching him caused him to start biting again and, just as I was getting hold of him, he bolted out of his hole. He circled the inside of the window well until I caught him and shoved him in the box. Laura, shaking, slapped on the screen.

We raced up the stairs and outside before he thought to eat through the cardboard, or the screen for that matter. I put a limestone rock on the screen and got a drink to settle my nerves.

"Better just sit tight," the hog must have thought, huddled in a corner, steeped in misery, shock, and fear.

Then I potted the hog in a large pot from Mexico made out of baked clay an inch thick. It already had dirt in it to make it homey, and I added water and grass for nourishment. Once I had him potted, we sat there for a while to see what would happen. Could he, for instance, eat right through such a pot? No, but almost immediately he tried to knock the screen off the top, so I had to weigh it down with more pieces of limestone. In his efforts, the hog quickly muddied up his water and himself.

I began to ponder the notion of making a pet out of the pitiful creature. Groundhogs do make good pets, I had heard, though not the indoor type that you'd have a special pillow on the couch for. I had the idea that having an undomesticated animal for a pet might give me a glimpse of life not yet completely cultivated by human civilization.

So for several days I nursed the hog, who came to be called Junior, with milk from a baby bottle. He liked the milk, but never once acted like he cared for me. Finally, I dabbed a spot of white paint on the top of his head—to tell him from four other little hogs now grazing in the yard—and let him go. My theory was that if any sort of bonding had gone on, Junior would grow up to be a friendlier hog than the others in the brood. Time would tell, I thought.

Meanwhile, life went on. Since the kitchen didn't have a garbage disposal, and we seemed to be having a lot of ever-hungry visitors around now, we started pitching everything left on the table into the backyard. I won't say that it was a bad idea—I still do it, anyway—but within days we had families of raccoons and opossums coming right up on the deck, taking over. Almost all young animals are appealing, even opossums after they're past the red, naked, thumb-sized stage, but animal mothers can be just terrible, ready to snap at you over any little thing, so we had to watch it.

We really had to watch out for Sweet William, the skunk who came to visit every few days. Sweet William was one of the most unconcerned, oblivious creatures I have ever met, moving in a slow, dawdling swish, sniffing everything, but seeming not to see anything at all. Once, he and Laura met head-on by accident behind the garage and both stopped, but Sweet William's tail went straight up just to signal who had the right-of-way. The little skunk was totally fearless, and had been even back in the days of Esme and Big Dog. I guess they all are, since it must take the most desperate of predators to pay such a price for what has to be a bad meal anyway. I got whiffs of Sweet William every now and then, and prayed that of all our candidates he wouldn't be the one to move into the window well. Then one day I found his home on the northeast corner of the property, a big smelly hole he's still living in even as I write.

We also had more little cottontail rabbits than we ever were able to estimate living along the drainage ditch by the road, loafing during the day and coming out at dusk to forage. Once, a box turtle with a high-domed and colorful carapace passed through, coming from the nature preserve on his way to the ridgeline. He was about the size of my cap, and seemed almost tame during the few minutes I manhandled him. Not long after, we grabbed a beautiful red and green and brown and yellow painted turtle, but he didn't seem tame at all; he writhed free and ran for Snake Lake like a sea turtle running for the ocean. Then we met a giant black rat snake which, I'm ashamed to say, I murdered out of ignorance, thinking it was poisonous. Later I learned what a friend to man they are, living on rats and other disagreeable vermin.

But by far, we saw more white-tailed deer than anything, sometimes six or seven or more at a time, usually at night, but sometimes at dusk when they stopped at the apple orchard down the road on their way to where they slept in the woods behind my house. They've been around here for some time, but their numbers increase every year. One night when Eddie was helping me take garbage cans out to the road, we suddenly were surrounded by a herd so close that we could feel the air move as they thundered away like a band of wild horses.

Another night, we heard howling and yapping and yipping coming from the nature preserve, and nobody took me seriously when I said I thought we were hearing coyotes. They hadn't been seen around here in years. I had no answer for that, but I had grown up listening to Texas coyotes and could never forget the hellish sound once they really got their bonding rituals going. Then I ran into some neighbors who raised exotic chickens for show. They told me that one morning around eight, when the chickens were let out to graze, a coyote who had obviously been lying in wait pounced and gobbled up several prize-winning chickens. He had good taste, too, selecting the delicate little Chinese varieties, the kind with feathers on their feet. That turned out to be the first official sighting of a coyote in Delaware County in five years, but the wildlife management people told my neighbors they felt sure the animals had never stopped slinking around here completely. Now they were making a real comeback.

One day Laura ran inside the house with a Jefferson salamander, named after Thomas Jefferson, our third president and an accomplished naturalist. We put it in a plastic watering pot that had a long thin spout. Laura thought she had discovered a worm with legs. It was a big one, about six inches long, and seemed frozen. But when we came back to look at it later, planning to let it go, it had apparently thawed because it was already gone, having escaped up the nozzle. It had left part of its tail, though, which wiggled for hours. We hunted for the tail-less Jefferson, but never found it.

After that, I kept my eye open for more of those eerie salamanders. I was engaged by their shy manner. Most creatures seem to feel that they have a place on this planet, and in one way or another they let you know it, especially the more social species like people and birds and many frogs. But the salamander is mute and retiring, living under rocks or in mud or water. It is such an elusive animal that most people have never seen one. They can be quite beautiful, though, in their own slimy, wiggly way. Laura was right. They do look like snakes or worms with legs—or lizards without skins. They are cold and sticky to the touch. Young ones I've seen are dark in color and seem not to have hind legs. Salamanders have lives of their own, of course, with courting and a few other social activities. But they are so secretive that I think they know they're two hundred million years out of date, and fear that their days may be numbered.

I was equally taken with the insect life around us, but in a different kind of way because they were such a plague. There was far too much insect life, as far as I was concerned, but a few of them stand out as real individuals.

There was, for instance, an eight-spotted forester—a moth that to me looks more like a butterfly—that began to get aggressive with me, the way a mosquito does. It flapped erratically around my head, then began perching on parts of my body such as my hand and bare knee. Even though I acted annoyed and even swatted at it, the moth kept dabbing its proboscis around on my skin, fast, as if it were really gobbling something up. I tried to let it have its way since it wasn't hurting me, but I just didn't like the feel of that wet little proboscis. Finally I went inside. The eight-spotted forester hung around the back screen door for a while, then left. I still don't know what it was eating off of me that it liked so much.

Conversely, I take a kind of perverse pride in not being afraid of the various kinds of Hymenoptera. I like to act as if nothing is going on when a bee or hornet sends my visiting friends racing into the house, screeching, "Kill it! Kill it!"

There is a yellow ground wasp I don't like, though, and haven't ever since they swarmed me the year before Eddie and the family came. They're too aggressive, even away from their hole in the ground, acting as if they might just sting you for the wine in your glass if they were in the mood.

So when I found a new hole full of them near where we made our camp fires on nice evenings, I decided to annihilate the nest. I was taking a chance because they attack every time you seriously menace their hole, but I somehow managed to stick the nozzle of a gasoline can inside without being stung, left it there, and let a gallon or so gurgle down.

Then I crept back, took the can away, and lit a match. It was wonderful to watch the flame come out of the hole, burning like a candle for over a half hour, while fifty or so wasps helplessly circled it. But when the fire went out, they just resumed use of their now-blackened entrance.

I got the hose, stuck it in the hole and ran water until it flooded, which took a surprisingly long time. But soon after I took out the hose, the water settled into the earth beneath or around the nest, I suppose, and the wasps started using the hole again.

Exasperated, I got a log off the woodpile and put it over the hole. That would do it, I was certain, but a couple of days later I saw wasps still around the log. I checked and found that they were going down in a dozen other little holes all around the big one. Furious, I emptied a whole giant-sized spray can of Yardguard on the holes, and that got some of them, all right—but not enough to matter, I guess, because they're still here today.

With some distance, and in the abstract I must admit, I really admire such creatures because of their ability to survive. The fact is, most creatures that threaten us or that we dislike are successful. Maybe that's why we dislike them.

All this life had an effect on me that will never go away. I was sitting in my office, wondering what I might want to write about next, and I wondered why not life itself? I knew it was a good idea—the only question was, would it sell? Besides animal life, there was plant life. Human life. Rich life. Poor life. Intelligent life. Life after death and life in outer space. It all seemed connected, too. I even imagined I could see a connection between early comets and the frogs Eddie was perusing in Snake Lake. After studying Halley's Comet, scientists believe that some comets do contain organic molecules, and that if enough of them had landed in the primordial soup of earth, they really could have given rise to life itself.

I was still just a dreamer, though, and if I ever felt too secure in my imaginative conclusions, Laura could easily shake me with a question like, "What makes light go so fast?"

"We'll ask your father," I said to that one, but it was galling to think that I not only didn't know but had never thought to ask. As I got to know Laura better, I was beginning to think that she was smarter than I, which could have been demoralizing, but instead made me want to share everything with her, to help her become, perhaps, another Margaret Mead. That was the way a doting father might think, I realized, and to me she probably really was the child I never had. During the spring Laura was on Winter Road, she came to represent the future. The hope which that gave me helped bring the present to life in a way I had never quite felt before.

Harley Warrick, Mail Pouch Barn Painter
Barkcamp State Park ©Becky Linhardt

CHARLENE FIX

CHARLENE FIX is an Assistant Professor of English at the Columbus College of Art and Design. She received an Ohio Arts Council Fellowship in · Poetry in 1993 and has published poems in *The Antioch Review*, *Negative Capability*, *Painted Bride Quarterly*, *Wind*, and *Crazy River*. She is the mother of three.

Somewhere during our lives, we meet an individual on the periphery of life, an obscure person who the rest of the world can forget, but we can't. Dino is such a person. "In Memory of Dino" is a character sketch of an unassuming and unpredictable shoe store repairman in Columbus, Ohio, who used to stay away from his shop for several days in a row and rarely fixed a person's shoes until the second or third visit. "Once he did the work," Charlene Fix writes, "he did it well." Through attention to detail and poignant observations, Fix puts a "human face" on Dino that makes him unforgettable to her and to us.

IN MEMORY OF DINO

I first did business at Dino's Shoe Repair when my husband, baby daughter, and I moved back to Columbus in 1975 from Atlantic City. We left behind gambling referendums, *Monopoly* streets, a diving horse, and other boardwalk anachronisms. We left the salt and waves always at the periphery of hearing, sight, smell and taste to return to Ohio's hills and valleys, trees and farms, cities and towns. We had come back for graduate school, and in those days had a car that broke down frequently and little money, so we walked a lot and wore down many soles and heels.

Dino's Shoe Repair was handy, though his hours were unpredictable. Sometimes when the shop should have been open, it would be dark and deserted. The jeweler next door must have gotten tired of answering the questions of people wanting their shoes, so he installed a lock on his door—he said, because of crime. Anyway, you had to ring a bell and a buzzer would sound to open the jeweler's door, a sensation like shaking hands with a hand buzzer trickster. That extra ordeal to find Dino dissuaded most, who instead would try his door, shrug, then come back the next day. The shoemaker's absence was one of those things over which you had no control, something not in sync with your life. This time that something had a human face.

A face with a history no doubt—Dino was a brown skinned man of about forty-five or fifty with neatly trimmed hair and unblinking round eyes. I wonder now if he was a veteran of World War II or the Korean War, or maybe the private war that members of minority groups sometimes fight. He always seemed distracted in spite of his surface composure. He neither smiled nor frowned, and spoke with an unfailing politeness when he informed the people, who came for their tired old shoes overlaid with new life, that their shoes weren't ready yet.

For this was the cost of doing business with Dino by the time I started coming to his shop: he often didn't fix your shoes. You'd come back two or three times, and finally, if you asked him to fix them while you waited, he would. Once he did the work, he did it well—his repairs were cheap and they lasted. That may be why he had customers, but I think that Dino gratified another need. You couldn't procrastinate with your family or job, but you could be stunned and pleased to watch Dino walk away from that Sisyphean mound of shoes, a labor that would take him longer than he had in this life. He would go to the Salvation Army store near his shop to putter among old watches or well thumbed books, where, as the jeweler pointed out to me once, you could find him if you really had to have your shoes. So I guess you had to have a philosophical bent to take your shoes to Dino: you could see that he was bearing up under the strain of having too many things to remember to do. You were refreshed when he took some air.

Dino's shop was as textured as his face, as interesting as his character. He had old *National Geographics* stacked high, and a radio always tuned to PBS, discussions or classical music filling the wondrous silence that enveloped him. His big dog, a Shepherd type, was always with him there, sampling with nose and tongue whomever came through the door, going back and forth greeting those who entered and perhaps scaring some away, then sashaying back behind the counter, into the denser atmosphere of leather, glues, and oils, to sit by his man.

You could enjoy being in Dino's shop, listening to his quiet firm tones with which his dog always complied, if you could remain calm about the puzzled customers with their meaningless claim checks who came for their shoes. For Dino's system was nonexistent. Once he actually bent over and took up an old claim check from the floor and gave it to me. Of course there was no matching one tied to my shoe. He just thought I might expect a number, and part of me did: the part that was habituated to dry cleaners, bakeries, and customer service counters, other shoe repair shops, income tax, social security. But the other part of me, the Harpo part wanting to honk in assent that life's moments, like flocks of multicolored birds, defy being numbered and contained, the part loving the chaos that mirrors that flight, even the part rendered wordless before the mystery and sorrow in the human face, loved Dino for handing me that widower claim ticket, the correlative of all the vanished moments I had walked through in those shoes.

One winter the rubber heels came off my boots so I took them to Dino. At that time his shop was exceptionally cold—he had no heat and couldn't fix my boot heels because his glue was frozen too thick to apply. I see more in this now. He was not paying his bills, was forgetting to or could not. Perhaps he had lost his less long-suffering customers, the ones who did not see that they were fellow riders on the wheel. Nevertheless, I really needed my boots. That winter was dumping a lot of snow on Columbus, and I was sloshing through it in increasingly soaked shoes. After several trips to Dino and my boots not repaired because the glue remained frozen—we seemed locked in this conundrum—he struck upon the happy plan to take the glue home overnight to a place where he had heat. I don't remember if my boots were to go home with him too. I think not. Rather, the glue, warm from a night wherever Dino laid his head, would be syrupy enough to do the job first thing in the morning, before it, or his intentions, got all clogged up again.

So it was that my boots were eventually repaired. By then the snow had stopped falling, and I had walked miles feeling the cold and wet slowly infiltrate my shoes and work its way through my socks. I experienced the shock of hot feet meeting the elements, was reacquainted with the bone-chill death that winter is. I marveled that bakers still made bread, that truckers could muster the vitality to screech around corners, spraying dirty slush on me.

The heels that Dino glued lasted forever. They never so much as budged away from the boot again, even though I pivoted often in my need to go separate ways, though I slipped and caught myself on treacherous patches of ice hiding beneath the March thaw, though now and again my own body betrayed me, my ankle running parallel to the earth. In fact, the boots disintegrated around those steadfast heels. The facade of vinyl peeled from its mesh form, flaking little by little, then falling in outright strips, and the mesh gave way to the world.

In fact, all of Dino's repairs lasted so long that I eventually lost track of him. I had learned to ask if he could fix my shoes right then, wait until he was through, and amuse myself by reading his old magazines or studying the arched back of the twelve o'clock cat advertising rubber heels. Once I even contemplated the little pile of used but respectably polished pairs of shoes for sale, shoes (Dino's scrawled sign told) that customers had never claimed. Then, shod dependably for a stretch of time, I didn't notice when his shoe repair shop closed for good. I swear I had just seen him poking through a pile of stuff at the Salvation Army store. And a few times I saw him walking with his dog in the parking lot of the grocery store near his shop. Once I even encountered him way out of the neighborhood, miles and miles north, and wanted to wave a hearty hello—ahoy, neighbor!—but I wasn't sure he would know who I was. By the time I wore down yet another pair of heels, his shop was empty and Dino gone.

There is no shoe repair shop close to where I live now, so I take my shoes wherever I may be about town. I have been to shops north, west, east and south. I always mention Dino in case shoe repair people know one another. And sometimes they do. One repairman told me that Dino's place must have been a front. One didn't know too much. One didn't seem to care. But I saw a man today who knew all about him. He fixed the broken clasp on my purse in a shop neat and bright as a pin, well stocked with shoelaces and boot creams on even rows of metal hooks. He had large windows, nice upholstered chairs, and a coffee table hosting a variety of recent magazines. His services were posted on crisp painted signs and even animated by a marquee of flowing red computer script repeating things we should have done to our shoes, making me think, in fact, that at that very moment

I was wearing shoes with heels worn down to the quick, though I couldn't leave them because then I'd have to go home in my socks. This shoe repairman said he did know Dino, that Dino didn't just close up shop. Dino died.

"Why?" I asked. "What happened?"

"Time," he said, "time and the place. His shop became the world to him." Time got to him, and all that he worked around.

Grays Armory, Cleveland ©Charles Cassady Jr.

DAVID CITINO

DAVID CITINO is Professor of English at The Ohio State University. A native of Cleveland, he received the M.A. and Ph.D. from Ohio State and taught at the Marion Campus of O.S.U. for eleven years before moving to Columbus in 1985. He is the author of seven acclaimed books of poetry including *The Appassionata Lectures* (1984), *The Appassionata Doctrines* (1983, 1986), *The Gift of Fire* (1986), *The House of Memory* (1990), and *The Discipline: New and Selected Poems* (1992). Among his honors and awards are a Poetry Fellowship from the National Endowment for the Arts, the first annual Kraut Poetry Award from the Ohioana Library Association and the Alumni Distinguished Teaching Award from Ohio State. He serves currently as Poetry Editor of O.S.U. Press and President of the Board of Trustees of Thurber House. Citino lives in Upper Arlington with his wife and three children.

"Somewhere (and by that I mean somewhere distinctive) the poet must dwell, and abide," writes David Citino in "My State of the State/Address." Ohio is the distinct place for him. Using an autobiographical approach, Citino explains how he's been "shaped (like the state itself, naturally and artificially), formed, reformed and informed" by living in Ohio. In doing so, he is able to discover where he is and, more importantly, who he is.

MY STATE OF THE STATE/ADDRESS

For approximately twenty-five years I've been writing—as writers like to say—*seriously*. Over this quarter-century I've situated my poems in such far-off locales as Calabria, Dublin and Galway; Paradise, Purgatory and the Inferno; the mountains of Colorado and Wyoming and the banks of an icy stream just outside Red Lodge, Montana; the labyrinthine, soul-haunted aisles of Vatican City, the Uffizi and King Tut's tomb; the dark caves of Neanderthal Europe and of small-town courthouses and bars; the wilderness of Sinai and the wilderness of the Northland Mall. Still, at the center of my work lies Ohio. This state is ever in my mind as a place nearly too real, a piece of land ("Round on the ends and Hi in the middle," as the Ohio State University Marching Band tells us) shaped like a sagging flag or a breast-plate made to fit a left-handed warrior, and looking not at all, I'm sorry to have to tell the Ohio Tourist Bureau, like a heart.

This land—shaped naturally by the graceful slope of Lake Erie to the north and the dancing meander of the Ohio River to east and south, and artificially by the uninteresting, perfunctory straight-edges of Indiana and Pennsylvania to the west and northeast, respectively—is the land of my birth, the place that brought me to my senses. It's like being nowhere else.

I've been shaped (like the state itself, naturally and artificially), formed, reformed and informed (and I hope not too terribly deformed) by Ohio. Often I've sought to capture in my poems the places (most of them on a scale of urban gray, as opposed to greenly rural) where I and my family have lived: Cleveland, to the industrial northeast; Athens, nestled in the green-hilled southeast; Columbus, smack-dab in the earnest middle; Marion, a fading, powdered north-central dowager still filled with pride from the days, ages away, when she ruled the world from the front porch of Warren G. Harding, yet still haunted by the fact that she is also the mother of Norman Thomas; Westerville, an island of W.C.T.U. temperance in a sea of indulgence; and Upper Arlington, where the middle class grazes, more or less contentedly.

Here, daily, I'm put in my place. The *Where* of it all, to me, adds up to *Who*, *what*, *when* and *why*. Or to put it another way, I can begin to answer the question "Who am I?" by fixing my position under specific constellations that come by to visit regularly, and seeking to determine, as accurately and completely as I can, the answer to the question, Where in the world am I?

Many are the writers whom place helps to define. Dickens is his London and Balzac his Paris; there are New Englands of Nathaniel Hawthorne, Emily Dickinson, Edwin Arlington Robinson, Robert Frost, Robert Lowell and (Ohio-born) Mary Oliver; Hardy is Wessex; Joyce's Dublin comes as close to the real thing as is humanly possible; Faulkner will live always in Yoknapatawpha County, a place as real as it is imagined; Californias are Robinson Jeffers and Robert Hass; Sherwood Anderson is Ohio, and so, at least on occasion, are James Thurber and James Wright.

A poet has come to be seen, at least since the Romantic period, as a winged figure mad enough to try to fly the highest heavens, azure realms where beautiful meets true, but while the poet often wishes to soar, or at least to walk about with head stuck in the clouds, he or she must on occasion have feet planted in something like native soil. The poet must be a resident of this universe, this galaxy, this solar system, this spinning planet, but for me that residency begins within a specific nation, state, county, city, precinct, ward—perhaps even a modest garden plot of tomato plants, onion, marigold, sweet basil, oregano and parsley, or a smaller plot of tooth and bone, marked by stone inscribed with a name and two dates. Somewhere (and by that I mean somewhere *distinctive*) the poet must dwell, and abide.

I remember, in Joyce's *A Portrait of the Artist as a Young Man* (a book which has had a strong influence on me, featuring a Dublin which I can understand and feel at home in because I was born and reared in religious precincts of Cleveland), how the young school-boy Stephen Dedalus, gazing at the earth in his geography book, fixes himself:

> Stephen Dedalus
> Class of Elements
> Clongowes Wood College
> Sallins
> County Kildare
> Ireland
> Europe
> The World
> The Universe

My version of that would involve rearranging Stephen's, the larger realms floating above and the smaller planted below, caught as an anchor is, with Ohio the thick chain holding it all together, in the middle, where Joyce places the Ireland from which he could never escape, even in exile. Ohio holds in place for me entities as small as elements and subatomic particles and as grand as the universe. To change the metaphor, Thoreau says, "If you have built castles in the air, your work need not be lost; that is where they should be. Now put the foundations under them." I've tried to dig my foundation in a state of history rich in human resources, water and land, acres and acres of rust and even, at times, a state that comes close to loveliness.

I don't consider myself a regionalist, and many of my poems move me to sites more distant and locales more exotic, such as those enumerated at the outset of this essay, but Ohio is my starting point and (in its diversity, its mix of rural and urban, White, Black, Brown, Red and Yellow, nature and the unnatural, the fortunate and less so, the pristine and the utterly despoiled), Ohio is my microcosm, my universe in miniature. The attention I pay to my state can give my poems—on those lucky occasions when I'm able to get one moving in the right direction—the particulars for every general, the here and now I need in order to try to say what I try to mean, and give "a local habitation and a name" even to the sweet by-and-by.

Often a poem of mine begins with that very attempt to capture a sense of this place. When I'm able to get down on paper the cry of a herring gull over the industrial Cuyahoga or the wings of it sisters bringing brightest dawn above the dam at Hoover Reservoir, the living shadows of ancient pines on the face of Lake Hope, shadows of telephone wires shimmering crazily in fetid Columbus puddles, shadows of power plant smokestacks bridging the grand and placid Ohio; the burial and ceremonial mounds of ruddy faced ones who lived here before and the sacred mound of soil in Cleveland Stadium the great Feller trod, and even the parched earth of my own sandlot scratchings; the rickety coal-tipples scaling precariously the hills of Vinton County and the furtive stills still hiding in hard-bitten hollers; the faces of my immigrant ancestors who rode in steerage from southern Italy and Slovakia to the shores of Erie, the faces of my own children, and the face of that callow St. Ignatius High School freshman leaning over the viscous Cuyahoga and then the Ohio University freshman staring intently up at himself from the flooded Hocking: at such times I can feel I've embarked on a journey worth the traveling. And isn't it true that all such journeys are journeys to and from home?

How often I ride the Memory Express to the Cleveland of my youth. Then the ethnicity of the place made it seem, even to the kid I was, a miniature Europe, what with neighborhoods of Italians, Poles, Irish, Hungarians, Slovaks, Slovenes, Croats, Ukrainians, Chinese and Jews—with their own places of worship, grocery stores, newspapers in the original tongue, and, of course, their own voluble ward-heelers and politicians. And although each group was often fiercely, obtusely intent on keeping to itself, even as the old neighborhoods broke up and folks took their photo albums and ceramic jockeys to the suburbs, I had friends named Bogomir and Mario and Moira and Patrick and Stanislaus and Irving. A close childhood friend from around the corner was Renaldo, Ronnie, a Gypsy.

And of course I knew then (as, sadly, I do even today) the balance of power, a truce ranging from uneasy to downright bloody, between neighborhoods of pure Black and White. A (Terminal) Tower of Babel, Cleveland seemed at times; at other times, though, I lived in a cosmopolitan city I could imagine as a New World Paris or Constantinople, one world encountering another on virtually every corner. It was as well a city with a world-class orchestra and art museum, and a political, industrial and social history that paralleled in so many ways that of the entire country.

I learned early on to respect an honest day's labor. Refineries and steel mills made the landscape lurid then. The stink of sulfur and coke and ash—not to mention the last slaughterhouse on the West Side—wafted through my bedroom window and over rusted ore carriers tended at the edge of Lake Erie by Hulett Unloaders, which still in my memory rise and fall, rise and fall like great black insects feeding, the operators riding into the very holds of ships to scoop out the precious ore, come from the Masabi Range and destined for the mills of Bethlehem and U.S. Steel. And of course the garlic, soy, cabbage, feta cheese, kraut, paprika, kielbasa sausage, steaming slabs of ribs with sweet, hot sauce, plates full of black-eyed peas, good and greasy greens.

We're told that our differences are melting away. Our speech, like our national cuisine, is becoming flat and indistinct. "In America, everything tastes the same," the Italian immigrant, newly arrived, would complain—and that was at the beginning of this century. It's more true today. Travel this land by plane, and the only difference evident is that little square of geography in the window a few minutes before take-off and landing, or, harder by far to appreciate, the speech of the flight attendants, or each and every cloud scudding by. Airports, like happy families, it seems, are all the same.

For me, however, Ohio is unusual enough to be real. Like Emily Dickinson's "certain slant of light," it operates deep inside, giving "internal difference/Where the Meanings, are." Such unsameness resides in the specifics of *where*.

Would I be able to argue that there is something so distinctly *Ohio* that I could tell by his or her writing or speech or dress that an individual hailed from here? Well, no. Kenneth Patchen and Mary Oliver and Rita Dove are all three distinct Ohio poets. Sherwood Anderson and Toni Morrison and Lee K. Abbott are diverse Ohio fiction writers. My landlord from Athens County with his Appalachian twang sounded nothing like my parents, with their Great Lakes nasalized way of speech. (To him, "Bob" was "B-awe-b," and outside the door there grew a "boosh;" to them, the proper names Ann and Ian were pronounced the same.) In Southern Italy, the language sounds strange to me, because the Calabrian dialect I heard in my youth was spoken with a Cleveland accent.

Music and writing were polyphonous, I learned early. As a young man with a guitar, I thought nothing incongruous about trying to sound Black when I sang the blues, "Ahm a jelly-roll bakah,/I bake da best jelly roll in town," or trying to put the tear in my voice when I did my Hank Williams: "I dreamed about Mama last night."

In my travelling life, almost always the time spent in places like Italy and Ireland has excited me to serious writing. Who knows where the rest of my life will take me? Still, it's here in Ohio where I've chosen to take my stand. In the deepest part of my sensibility a river meanders under bridges that rise and fall as if to greet it, the river enters a vast lake at a place where a city rises, a place of diversity of creed, culture and thought, and an urban yet celestial music rises, conducted by George Szell.

I was changed by my high school, brought out of the confines of the neighborhood. Taught by witty and urbane and terribly bright (and sometimes terribly cynical) men, most of them Jesuits, I began to see that in music and art and literature—and a major city—there are things to learn and desire beyond cars, football and baseball. I'd like to think that I've become a better writer and teacher than I was a middle linebacker and fullback, or southpaw sandlotter. The jury is still out on that. While most of the emphasis in this high school was on law and science and business—on raising up for the Roman Catholic urban middle class the leaders of the 21st century, attorneys, engineers and purchasing agents—writing was respected, literature read and taken to heart.

The young man I wanted to be, who thought himself so sophisticated, next found himself in another world entirely—although the same state. Athens was country and Appalachian and yet in every sense a university town, all lush green hills and Colonial architecture of Ohio University. I went hairy (after wearing for four years what the Jesuits described as "a neat, businessman's haircut") and Bohemian ("artsy," the term was then), beginning to carry around a Gibson guitar and a slim sheaf of slim poems. In Athens I met a woman, from the West Side of Columbus but with roots in Mississippi, who would collaborate with me on a life. Our favorite date for three years was to walk out into the dark countryside, traveling roads that wound their way beneath a hundred times more stars than I could see from my Cleveland backyard.

My present home, Columbus, was for years the largest city in the state in area and is now the greatest in population—although when the metropolitan area is considered, Cleveland is significantly more populous. Columbus is in many respects new—not unlike a Sunbelt city (but without the sun, sadly) in the way it has grown—its wealth coming from government and education, insurance and computers. What with Ohio State University and the colleges nearby, institutions like Thurber House (the writers' center located in the restored boyhood home of James Thurber in downtown Columbus), more large bookstores than you could shake sticks at, and the active and far-seeing Ohio Arts Council and Greater Columbus Arts Council, central Ohio has become something of a center of literary activity. The ethnic and cultural diversity is here, although not in the large doses enjoyed by Cincinnati and Cleveland, Toledo and Youngstown.

So, I've grown more or less comfortable in this state of cornfields and super-computers, achingly gentle hills and a shallow but nevertheless great lake. I may not be certain what or where I am, but the seeking after an answer close to home brings me closer to knowing. "An Ohio writer."—I like the sound of that, for all the limitations it suggests and all the teasing I must endure from colleagues who hail from the Bronx or New Mexico, Santa Barbara or Vienna. The poet Philip Levine once told me at a dinner, a smile on his lips, that he tried to imagine a place where poetry couldn't be written, and came up with Akron. He ribbed me throughout the meal about my Cleveland roots—and this from a poet from, of all places, Detroit!

No matter. This is a state of energy—although certainly not the boundless bounty the early settlers encountered, clear teeming streams, skies dark with bird, mile upon mile of timber, deer so thick that each tree seemed to hide meat enough for weeks. Still, even after centuries of development, phosphate lakes, waste-laden rivers, played-out veins of coal, the unearthly cobalt blue glow of Lake Hope and the coppery sheen of nearby streams gleaming from mine-slag, still it is a state of undeniable opportunity.

Following the Indians who found it and named it and then had it taken from them by force, treachery and disease, I can say along with the poet James Wright of Martins Ferry, in his poem "Beautiful Ohio":

> I know what we call it
> Most of the time.
> But I have my own song for it,
> And sometimes, even today,
> I call it beauty.

Where am I? Here. Nowhere else. I've seen, in my years, the truth and justice of Wright's qualified reckoning, and his honest appreciation of this place: "Most of the time," and "sometimes, even today," in trying to sing my song I call this beauty *Ohio*.

The Flats, Cleveland ©Charles Cassady Jr.

AMY SPARKS

AMY SPARKS is a poet, essayist, story writer, critic and editor living in Cleveland, Ohio. Sparks has distinguished her diverse career with an Ohio Arts Council Individual Artist Fellowship and associate editorship of Cleveland's *Free Times* and the Midwest *dialogue magazine*. As a performance poet, she has represented Cleveland in national poetry slams in Boston, Chicago and San Francisco. The springs of her mother's farming heritage in Chardon and her father's birth in Lima come together in their family's growing up in the Cleveland suburb of Rocky River.

This essay is an intimate portrait of her father and herself as the family survives his stroke. As she cares for her father as a parent now, she also learns anew the struggles and inspirations of his life. Mixing work and recreation, obligation and dreams, she senses the significance of one man's life. The writing is crafted to an openness of image and feeling, as she sings the true song of their life.

STRIKE

My father is learning to walk. He has managed to fall only once, climbing into his high white bed. He is practicing his handwriting, signing over and over again the name he's had for sixty-six summers. Every day he works his mouth into answers to questions like *Why are windows made of glass?*

I have learned odd things from him lately: During a storm off Guadalcanal the Navy cook made pork chops for luck; the best martinis come straight from the freezer in a bottle of gin with a capful of vermouth; my mother stopped eating for a while, confusing everyone.

My father is a dreamer who has encouraged me to buy an accordion just for the hell of it. A stockbroker for forty-two years, he still bets the horses and the lottery and never made a dime with the money of anyone he loved.

My father is a sailor who has never owned a boat. He used to crew on the broad face of Lake Erie—the spinnakers a line of handkerchiefs against the sky. My father is a sailor who watched his younger brother die of a heart attack on the same lake, sailing. He was thirty years old and my family, for the first time, kissed tragedy.

He belongs to every book-of-the-month club, never sends anything back and therefore has to pay for them. He has subscriptions to *Trout, Fly Fishing, Field and Stream*, and dozens more which mushroom around his bed. He buys $300 coins which he throws into drawers he may never look in again. He is waiting for things to mature, for his return, for his and our lives to come due. With interest.

He was going to retire, carefully studying books on how to tie flies for trout. Now all he wants to do is sit in the courtyard he laid with bricks two decades ago, surrounded by pots of lemon thyme, tangled day lilies announcing their short lives, and massive roses. He wants to listen to jazz, to Billie Holiday, and let the sun bake his eyelids shut.

His fragility has come full circle. We grew up in a house full of weeping faucets, incontinent refrigerators, loopy clocks, fuzzed-out radios, green-people

TV's, a long intricate dance of cars back and forth to the shop, a gas grill that blew up, a door that hasn't locked from the outside in 25 years, my father wholly unable to decipher the logical marriage of mechanical parts to themselves. We grew up believing our house a target of fate, that we were strangers in a land of mechanical breakdown. The machines spoke a new and clickety language; it was a mutiny of parts which picked on us precisely because we were so ineffective. We grew up believing in environmental anarchy, swearing at inanimate objects. When all along we wanted to break each other with terrible love, the machinery broke instead, and we were left kicking at metal.

Obsession, not mechanics, drives my father. A dark, spotted creature, the hyena among birds, has seized his imagination. Wooden loon decoys, painstakingly painted with tiny white flecks and long green swaths dotted with red glass eyes fill his den. There are books with pale watercolor plates of loons, loon country videotapes and recordings of their calls.

The year my mother died we took 1,200 pounds of gear, one husky dog and a boatload of grief to the camp in Quebec where the men in my family have been fishing and swigging whiskey for decades. In usual fashion we broke both the water pump and the outboard motor. But every night at dusk my father slipped to the edge of the lake, and proceeded with eyes closed, to call in the loons.

Every year the better part of this century the men have fled the city to the mysteries of barely charted Quebec. The rituals are set: beer before breakfast, whiskey for lunch with trout, and a London broil cooked over an outside grill, dropped in the sand at least twice before eating. Walleye, shore lunches, rude Frenchie jokes and no women. Moose sometimes and rancid butter, but that was in the old days. Over the door of the cabin hangs a photograph of my father's father knee-deep in a Quebecois cove, forehead tanned by afternoon waits for pike, a record one swinging from his hands like a disembodied thigh.

Defenseless against fads, my father let us twist and shout to new 45 records, take pictures of the sofa with Brownie cameras, wear Mickey Mouse watches to bed. One Christmas we descended at dawn to a choked living room, wall to wall with Batman caves, granny dresses, delicate china horses, Barbie and Ken, B.B. guns and two live rabbits named for foods. At the time we could all fit into the big Naugahyde chair, now splayed at the seams and covered with magazines. We watched "Lassie" on Sunday nights, ate Jiffy-Pop popcorn and listened to sonic booms peal down our roof.

I used to tiptoe to the kitchen and join him for a dead-of-the-night milk, his stomach churning with Dow Jones Industrials, mine with the thought of summer. He gave me a plastic guitar and taught me "Chinese" music by plucking beyond the bridge.

He has a perfectly named ailment: stroke. The stroke of a pen, of a swimmer slicing water. The stupid stroke of luck, as if God could still strike us down in the late twentieth century. It went like this: He goes for hotdogs at the seventh-inning stretch. The last time the Indians won a pennant he was a cocky G.I. Bill student back east, sending his laundry home on the train, a sorry bundle my grandmother met willingly at the station. There's a pop-up to left field, the sound of a train, my father facing everywhere but home. *It's a error.* There's a scramble in the upper deck. My father goes foul, the ground tilting beneath. Impact. Cheering. He's out.

Taking baby steps back to his seat, the air felt like tiny razors in his throat. He mumbled and brushed his new girlfriend away. The Indians were three games out of first.

This time the AWOL soldier clot got fat and happy before pushing off into the stream of red memories—sailboats, the stink of marigolds, dry jokes and small Ohio towns, countless dawns and four chords on the piano.

His best friend Bob was struck down last year, worse, leaving him chairbound and speechless, except for the odd ability to swear. We take my father to see him— old fishing buddies, sure pike-hunters rising with the mists off Six Mile Lake. Bob wags his good hand in greeting, yelling, "Dammit, dammit, dammit, dammit," fast and loud, an incantation meaning, "Hello, how the hell are you, you son of a bitch, can you believe the shape we're in?"

My father grabs his hand, leans in close, plots the next fishing trip in the spring while the women who tend these men stand by, incredulous. "Geezus Christ, gee-zus Christ," says Bob, meaning, yes. Oh yes.

We have never been able to pin down which small Ohio town my father's family came from—DeGraff, West Liberty, Lima, Bucyrus, crooked crossroads that flowered before Hitler was born. Sparks is from the Welsh, shortened from "sparrow-hawkers"—leather-fisted men who tended hunting birds. It's a name now without use, without bite. My father's father was a dandy who escorted girls in his carriage at dusk to Indian Lake. A giant of a man who lived high and died broke, after marrying the granary owner's only daughter. Her name was Nelle and she grew up in a huge Queen Anne on Main Street in Lima, a woman who went to college before women could vote, and had a special purse for her impromptu winnings at craps. These things my father tells me slowly, as if he is surprised I don't remember them.

Now he swings his bad arm like a heavy beam, and wraps his lips around carrots and peas, orange jello and clean white straws. I see him every day. The tomatoes have long since been stolen from his garden, and my sister has harvested all the herbs. Childless, I take his hand, childlike and curled. He bursts into tears, giggles and asks for the stock reports. I hold his arm as he takes shaky steps in his new shoes. It is unclear why windows are made of glass.

He wants never to have to tie shoelaces again, having asked for shoes that close with teflon...meaning velcro. But, and to him this is no contradiction, he would like to learn to tie flies for trout. He has told the nurse. She has her orders.

Recently I dreamed of babies gurgling beneath the surface of a freshwater lake. He stands on the bank, his line buzzing with flies. As he arcs his good arm back, the line snakes into a sign over the water. He teaches me how to reel in the past and press it into his bad hand like coins, to call in the birds who laugh at the moon.

Municipal Stadium, Cleveland ©*Charles Cassady Jr.*

LES ROBERTS

LES ROBERTS has been an actor, a professional musician and singer, and a businessman as well as a producer, lecturer and writer. He taught at U.C.L.A. and Glendale Community College in Los Angeles before moving to Cleveland in 1990, where he writes regular columns for the Cleveland *Plain Dealer*. A Chicago native, Roberts has authored several novels, including *An Infinite Number of Monkeys*, which won the "Best First Private Eye Novel Contest" in 1986. In 1988, he wrote his first book about Cleveland P.I. Milan Jacovich, *Pepper Pike*, followed by *Full Cleveland* (1989), *Deep Shaker* (1991), and the *Cleveland Connection* (1993). A fifth Milan novel—*The Lake Effect*—has just been published by St. Martin's Press, New York. In 1992, Roberts received the Cleveland Arts Prize for Literature and is currently the president of the Private Eye Writers of America.

After twenty-some years of living in the sun, fun and glitter of Hollywood, why would anyone pack up and head to Cleveland? That's what Les Roberts' L.A. friends wanted to know when the writer moved to Ohio in 1990. In "Ohioan By Choice," Roberts explains how and why he came to live in and love Ohio. Written from the perspective of an outsider turned insider, the essay examines one man's "enchantment with Ohio" and what he has discovered about Cleveland and Ohio that makes even the weather tolerable.

OHIOAN BY CHOICE

I'm a novelist, specializing in mysteries—what they call "hard-boiled," schweetheart. Maybe you've read one of my books. I hope so, because people reading me is how I make my living. There are those who still ask me, "Do you work?" because I don't "go to the office" every morning; my office is wherever I want it to be, as long as there's an outlet in which to plug my computer. I can live anyplace I like. My publishers don't care where the manuscript is postmarked.

I've lived all over the world—Chicago, where I was born and where I still thrill to the flags flying in the sunshine at Wrigley Field. New York City, specifically Greenwich Village back in the days when that meant artists and actors and poets, where I played out my young manhood and discovered who and what I was. New Mexico, with its mystical mountains and ski valleys and adobe and turquoise. Georgia, with its red clay and white verandas and barbecue pits redolent with the smoky odor of roasting pig. Exotic and sometimes dangerous Hong Kong, and for twenty-four years in Southern California, where I once possessed my own private parking place on the Paramount Studios lot and where I dined and dallied with show business legends.

I choose now to live in Ohio.

Call it karma, call it kismet, call it whatever you like, but there's been a buckeye brand on my flank since the moment I crossed the state line.

Like a second-time around love affair, my enchantment with Ohio began in my middle years. I had driven through it in my very green twenties, anxious to get where I was going and stopping only for coffee and the necessities, but my first real stay here was when I came from Los Angeles to do a three-month television job in January of 1987. I arrived with the attitude of a prisoner counting off the days on the wall of his cell. *Ohio*, I believed after two decades in La-La Land, was full of what the movie and TV industry calls "flyover people," i.e. the people they fly over while heading from one coast to the other to close a deal. Cleveland to them was a rust dump whose only *raison d'etre* was to fuel the monologues of late night comedians, and the rest of the state, now that Woody Hayes was gone, was right out of "Hee-Haw."

And it was going to be cold. I was used to arid Los Angeles, where they'd reclaimed the desert and built a city, where everyone displays a tropical tan and wears as few clothes as possible, the better to display it. Where they close the schools when it rains and break out the overcoats when the temperature drops below fifty-five degrees. It had been nearly thirty years since I'd seen it snow sideways, since I'd stepped in slush, since I'd had to bend my head into the teeth of a gale and be careful I didn't fall on my butt on the ice.

I wasn't looking forward to my Ohio stay.

But those negative feelings lasted only as long as it took to drive from Hopkins Airport through downtown Cleveland.

"That's one of the most beautiful buildings I've ever seen!" I said, peering out through a lightly-falling snow. "What is it?"

"Terminal Tower," my driver told me, and gave me a little bit of the building's history, pointed out the other bridges and Lake Erie and the smoke stacks of the steel mills just downriver in the belly of the Flats.

It was at that moment I began re-thinking my stay. This was going to be okay, I reasoned. It's one of America's major cities in one of its most populous states— and it's kind of pretty here. This might not be so bad.

The very next day I was driven downtown from my office in Beachwood, past some of the beautiful old houses of the eastern suburbs, the white snow on the lawns that sloped up to the front doors like the bright white stiff shirt of a butler. I could barely contain my excitement.

"It's been thirty years since I've seen a frozen pond!" I exclaimed, and was thrilled at the sight of it.

There were to be a lot of revelations over the next three months. The stunning architecture of Cleveland was built long ago by true artists and not bean-counters. In Los Angeles, any building pre-dating 1952 is torn down to make way for a strip mall with donut shops and video stores, but here structures three times that old remain and are treated with the respect and reverence they deserve—Gray's Armory, the Old Stone Church, the onion domes of the Byzantine cathedrals that startle the eye as you drive I-71. And that magnificent, too-big, too-drafty old Stadium on the lakefront where Bob Feller once stood atop the mound and glared batters into submission and where Jim Brown used to run through defenders so hard they never even remembered being hit, much less what hit them.

The wildness of Lake Erie stretched gray and cold to the furthest horizon like a lake on the surface of the moon. Lake Michigan in my native Chicago is a user-friendly sort of lake, but Erie, with its air of remote mystery, is twice as fascinating.

The two little old ladies waiting their turn in the Shaker Deli discuss in their heavy European accents the relative merits of Bernie Kosar and John Elway in an upcoming NFL Browns-Broncos playoff game. They didn't know much about football, but they knew from the brown-and-orange pompons and banners that had sprouted all over the city that something exciting was going on, something good for their neighbors, and they wanted to be a part of it. And so did the neighborhood tavern keeper who irreverently displayed a John Elway poster hung upside down behind his bar.

There were the neatly-kept and freshly painted older houses of Cleveland Heights, built to last seventy years earlier and fulfilling their promise.

The incredible natural beauty of the surrounding countryside—there is no more idyllic place on earth than the Chagrin River Valley, with its thick stands of oak and maple and catalpa, dotted with lovely Cape Cod Colonial homes that might have been there for two hundred years, and the occasional rolling pasture in which lovely horses strolled, watching the steam rise from their nostrils and feeling the exhilaration of the brisk cold. Of course my biggest treat would be seeing it in the fall where its colors rival that of New England.

The more the city receded in the rear-view mirror, the greater the impression Northern Ohio made on me: Geauga County with its maple syrup and its neat little town squares that I remembered from Andy Hardy movies when I was a kid. Amish Country with its quaint buggies and the solemn folks inside them with the merry twinkle in their eyes. Working farms blanketed with snow. The military flying formations of the Canada geese casting a shadow over the blue-gray sky.

One night coming home from a dinner party in Chagrin Falls, a deer bounded across the road in front of me, almost ghostly in the few milliseconds it remained in my headlights. In Southern California the kind of wildlife that runs in front of your car is generally in the country illegally or on their way to or from the commission of a crime.

Toto, we're not in Los Angeles any more, I thought. And I was glad.

Most different were the people. Ohioans are as loving and giving as any population I've met. Their warmth isn't the automatic and phoney have-a-nice-day politeness of Los Angeles, and it's light-years from the get-out-of-my-way-or-I'll-rip-off-your-face coldness of New York. It's genuine; Ohioans care about their neighbors, they care about other people, they are fiercely proud of their state and want to share its wonders with visitors. It took me a few weeks to realize that, unlike the milieu from which I'd just come, they weren't being nice to me because they "wanted" something, but because that's the way they are when a stranger enters their midst. When an Ohioan asks, "How are you?" he expects you to tell him—because he's genuinely interested.

When my job here was finished and it was time to go back to my California home, I felt an odd catch in the area of my heart. In my years in the TV industry I'd gone a lot of places, done what I'd had to do and said goodbye without a second thought. Leaving Ohio was a strange, sweet sadness.

But the hook was already in, and had dug deep. I thought a lot about Ohio when I got back to California. I made a point of drinking my morning coffee out of my Cleveland mug, a bon voyage gift from my friends in Cleveland, because it brought back such good memories. I recalled the meals I'd eaten in the Flats, watching the tugs and ore boats negotiate the ice-covered Cuyahoga River. I followed the fortunes of the Cavs, Browns, Indians, and Buckeyes with more than a passing interest, and talked about them so much that someone bought me an Indians jacket for my birthday.

I decided to set a series of mysteries in northern Ohio. Part of the choice was because Cleveland and its environs were largely unexplored in the mystery genre. Jonathan Valin had put Cincinnati on the mystery map with his fine Harry Stoner novels; I wanted to do the same thing for Cleveland.

I created a detective hero that was pure Cleveland. His name is Milan Jacovich, a Slovenian American who had gone to Kent State, served in Vietnam, and had all his roots on the ethnic East Side. As I wrote the first novel, which came to be called *Pepper Pike*, my love for the city and the region found its way onto the page.

Jacovich goes out to Gates Mills in the course of a murder investigation:

> The Chagrin River Valley is beautiful any time of year, but I prefer it in winter. The rolling hills and the naked birch and dogwood trees whitened by fresh snow, the gentle slopes dipping down to the ice-encrusted river, and the serenity and the stillness make the valley a favorite getaway of mine...The homes are all set back from the road on lots that are, by law, at least three acres, most often larger, and almost everywhere you look recalls a Currier and Ives Christmas print. It also seems a uniquely American place; winter woods in Austria or Switzerland might be just as lovely, but I'm sure they have a different feel. European. The Chagrin River is an American kind of river, the sort on which everyone wishes they had spent their childhood. It's an elegant place to be, never more so than in the snow, and despite the nature of my visit I was glad to have the occasion to see it in its winter clothes.
>
> (*Pepper Pike, 1988*)

The book became a regional best-seller in northern Ohio. When I came back in the fall on a book-promotion tour I saw my Ohio friends again. Nothing had changed—they were as kind and accepting as ever. I returned home and wrote a second Jacovich novel, *Full Cleveland*. Although I continued to write about Los Angeles too, there was just something about Cleveland. Like a bustling, industrialized Bali Hai, it called to me. I fantasized moving there, living in a white Cape Cod Colonial with a room to work in which afforded me a view of trees and grass and sky.

But that's crazy, my friends told me. Nobody leaves Los Angeles and moves to Cleveland!

In the spring of 1990, I found myself somewhat adrift. Divorced for many years, most of my family had moved out of Los Angeles, as had my two best friends. Los Angeles was becoming a difficult city in which to live—crime, racial tensions, killer smog, eighteen hour-a-day traffic gridlock, and a what's-in-it-for-me mindset that was at odds with my midwestern upbringing; in L.A. you either become one of the piranhas and feed on human gullibility, or you leave. The movie-TV industry and I had mutually turned our backs on each other, and after twenty-four years, I was ready for a change.

There has to be some reason to live in a place besides the weather.

Cleveland seemed to me to be just what I was looking for. It's a major league city. As culturally aware and aggressive as anyplace I've ever lived, it boasts one of the world's great classical orchestras, one of the finest art museums in America, a burgeoning jazz scene, a model library system, two superb ballet companies and a broad range of live theatre, concerts, lectures and film festivals. Fine restaurants range from the very trendy and very expensive to plain mom-and-pop places with mismatched chairs, serving a variety of satisfying ethnic foods. Within fifteen minutes of Public Square is an unspoiled countryside where you can still smell the grass grow.

And yet it would be out of the fast lane in which I'd lived and tried to hang on for more than two decades. There is a small-town feel to much of Greater Cleveland because of its wonderful neighborhoods. The city is manageable, accessible. After letting the sense of the place grow inside me for almost four years, I knew it was where I wanted to be.

So I contacted an Ohio friend who was in real estate and told her I was coming in September to look at houses.

I was terrified. Shakespeare said that we would rather bear those ills we have than fly to others we know not of, and even though I was no longer content with Southern California, Ohio was still largely unknown to me. Would I like it as much 365 days a year as I had on my brief visits? Would the support system of warm, welcoming people I'd met here, the new friends, hold on a day-to-day basis? Did I really want to leave a place where I'd lived for a decade to settle in a city where I had no roots at all?

I didn't know. Emerson observed that man could learn a lesson from the lowly tortoise, who never takes a step forward without sticking his neck out, and as a creative artist, all my life I had been a risk-taker. So I flew to Cleveland and began house-hunting.

The seventh house I looked at was a white Cape Cod Colonial with a second-floor sunroom overlooking Cain Park in Cleveland Heights, with a view of trees and grass and a large expanse of southern sky.

I'm writing these words in that room, looking out at the black skeletons of the winter trees against the gray sky. A bushy-tailed squirrel is busy doing what squirrels do. Last night one of my friends from that first visit to Ohio came to dinner, and I built a fire and we drank inexpensive wine and ate pasta with Feta cheese and listened to the rain the weather forecasters had threatened us with all day yesterday.

I've been here just over three years now, the happiest and most productive years of my life. I've seen parts of Ohio I'd never seen before, quaint little villages in the midst of lush farm country undulating its way over the nearest hill. Ethnic enclaves of Cleveland, where cultures from all over the world have blended into a city that is beginning to work again, one filled with beautiful faces that are black and brown and Slavic and Nordic. There is the stately campus of Ohio State in Columbus, academic excellence existing side-by-side with football mania; deer and raccoons, muskrats and ducks peeking out from woods in every conceivable shade of green.

I've met more than a thousand people here—and there were only two I didn't like. Many have become cherished companions, and a few of them good true friends. And I've published three more novels set in Ohio.

Sometimes I want to kick myself that it took me a large part of my life to discover Ohio. But there is a right time for everything, and apparently the right time for me to find where I belonged was on an evening in January of 1987 when the northern part of the state had gone ballistic because the Browns had just won a playoff game and the lights of Terminal Tower beckoned to me through a gently-falling snow.

Ohio styles itself "the heart of it all." I don't know about that—the heart finds its home in many places. I just know that mine is home here.

Spring Planting, Knox County ©*Becky Linhardt*

DIANE FENCL

DIANE FENCL grew up in Kent, Ohio, and it is the center of much of her work. A graduate of Kent State University in journalism and English, she now works as a writer at Spectrum Publications in Orrville, Ohio, and is contributing to a book on the history of Kent for the Kent Historical Society. Fencl also writes for *Inklings* magazine which attempts to record history as it is unraveling.

In this personal essay the author struggles with the family values of work vs. freedom. She poses two historical perspectives here in her portrait of her grandfather's farm and hard working values and her own contemporary life in the city of Kent where she finds meaning in simple enjoyment. Clearly the author wrestles with issues facing the people of Ohio, the Midwest, and the nation: What to do with our lives?

LAZY BONES

Every family has a well-kept secret and mine is no different. The secret is that we have the propensity in our genes to be lazy. Anyone who knows my grandfather (as many people in Portage County do) would look askance at the assertion and say, "Really?" And I would have to admit that idleness creeps in on my grandmother's side through the Rosies, who live in a run-down shack on Infirmary Road in Shalersville, with rusted tractors and old cars strewn in the yard. I would hardly know they exist, except for some inside family jokes of which I've become a part; yet, my fear is that my family, who strive by the Protestant work ethic, will one day discover that my generation, and that includes me, is lazy, too.

Of course, my grandfather, who is now 85, is a long yardstick for comparison. He grew up on a farm and dreamed he would be a farmer one day. As a boy, he would get up before the sunrise, milk his father's cows, walk two miles to work as a farm-hand at the Goodall's then walk home again at night, a long day's toil for the $1/day wages he was paid.

Eventually, his work ethic paid off. In the height of the Great Depression, he got a bank loan and purchased 122 acres with a house and a barn and has been active ever since. Sure, he told me there were days when he didn't feel like working, but he said he had no choice but to work, for his dream propelled him. Today, he rents his land, with beauteous maple trees spotting the fields and framing the Western Reserve style house, to other farmers who are making their toil. And looking back he'll say, "I always loved what I did for a living, always knew what I wanted to do." His way of life is passing by the wayside, though. Farmland around him is being built up with houses, and the county is building a jail across the street. My grandfather remembers yesterday, however, as though it were today. He got up plenty of his mornings at 4 a.m. to spray the potatoes or to tend a sick calf, so all in all he's been a happy man living in his paradise, the woods and fields he can call his own.

Yesterday, when my grandfather was recounting his success tale, my mother commented, "That's how you become a success." That's when I worried about the family secret. I thought of my cousin, Andrew, who takes a long nap after he wakes up at 6 a.m. to milk his dairy cows; I though of my cousin, Jim, who quit his first job out of college selling tires on commission in Akron because he wasn't making enough money, and it wasn't what he wanted to do (despite my grandfather's protestations that it's easier to find work when you have work); I thought of my cousin, Lori, who lies in the sun between jobs cleaning hotel rooms at the University Inn and is now a bronze goddess; I thought of my sister, Denise, who spends her days off as a stewardess hunting for antiques at Farnsworth's and rollerblading; and I thought of me, who would rather read a book in the Kent State Library than show up for a nine to five routine making an honest day's wage behind a desk at Spectrum Publications in Orrville.

Don't breathe a word of our laziness to my grandfather, though. He would be crushed. He lives by the yardstick of the old days when it wasn't unusual to walk five miles to a one-room schoolhouse in Freedom Township, come home to bail the hay and recite Latin in between helping with the meals that a sick mother could not make. I'll give you an example of just how out-of-touch my very intelligent grandfather can be: He thinks I can afford a 112-acre farmhouse on my wages of $16,000 a year. He has it picked out of the "Farm and Dairy" auction section, complete with cows, a white picket fence such as horses are penned into, and a front porch. "It would be a nice place, you could live with your sister and share the payments," he tells me, adding that he purchased his farm in the Depression and made it through. Well, times have changed. Frankly, I am not willing to take a second job and work from dawn to beyond dusk, as he did. I want time to read Muriel Spark, take a bike ride, watch for birds, and luxuriate in a long bubble bath.

In short, my generation questions the hard way of life of our ancestors. We have parents who have worked for 40 years in the same occupation at the same place of work. We've watched them come home to cook dinner, do the yardwork, and maybe watch the news. Increasingly, we discover that our college educations at Kent State University with its jumping black squirrels, are good for a low-wage, probably part-time job, with meager benefits. Still, we want the comforts we grew up with: the cable TV, the comfortable cars, the luxurious apartments, with as little toil as possible. One has only to listen to our choice of music to understand the rebellion: Pink Floyd's "We don't need no education," or perhaps Guns N' Roses,' "Nothing lasts forever but the cold November rain." Out outlook is, indeed, bleak.

As a child, I recall the comforts of home at my grandparents' farm in Shalersville. I would spend sunny days playing make believe that I was an Indian or a prairie settler at a campsite, then come inside to have my grandmother make popcorn, and we'd watch Lawrence Welk on TV. Wholesome smiles and sweet songs about a bicycle built for two, or "Go Away Little Girl,"" would make me teary eyed even then as I envisioned my home of the future. Now, a single 30-year-old, I go to sports bars, like Benny's Rubber City in Akron, where want-to-be athletes play ping pong and live their dreams by watching Hollywood basketball stars plug Reebok shoes on prime-time commercials. The sports fans love the excitement of watching Magic Johnson make a winning basket, but they've given up in their age of complacency in making it big themselves. They've succumbed to watching from afar, allowing the television to bring their dreams into a living sleep. The competition, the age of marketing, has made it too difficult for the average person to make a mark, and so we observe from our chairs as the world passes by. There simply isn't enough room for all of us to have it all. One can only go so far, and so our dreams dissipate.

I grew up in this university town, where I still live. Every day I watch over-grown students hanging on to youth and ideals. I go into Brady's Cafe for a cup of coffee and bump into Jen, a 31-year-old art student who sells magazine subscriptions part-time in downtown Kent. She has cable TV and spends her evenings watching "L.A. Law" and MTV. She promotes a local band, Dink, and drinks coffee with the band members during afternoons. She works evenings. When she comes home, she goes out to hear local bands at Ozzie's and J.B.'s on North Water Street, beds down around 3 a.m. and is up by 11 a.m. to work out at a gym she can't afford but can't give up, despite the due rent and eviction notices. She falls back on her liberal parents when money is tight, despite their warnings that she should be self-reliant. Jen is typical of many students who can't get beyond the college schedule, who get used to the flexibility that a day at school allows, who would rather be homeless than join the Establishment. Kent is full of carpenters and handymen who also enjoy a free life, one clear of too many responsibilities and a working day's commitment. There seems no greater feeling than to know you have the freedom to jet off to Europe or hang out in Toronto while the rest of the world is stuck in a rut. It's truly a feeling that you've somehow "beat the system."

My grandparents were always staunch Republicans. When I grew up, they expressed horror at government handouts and welfare abuse. "They spend all their money on beer and cigarettes," was my grandmother's plea against social welfare programs for the poor, as she looked with disapproval at the n'er do wells lining up for a free meal at The Center of Hope in Ravenna. Although I carried a lot of her views when I was in college, now I see things in a different light. I have a friend who is eking out a living with her restaurant, trying to raise a 4-year-old child. She works long hours, day and night, and yet she can hardly pay her restaurant's bills, let alone her personal ones. Whereas I used to view my grandfather with strict admiration and fondness, I now see that there was a certain amount of luck involved in his success. He had the brains to run a business so that it made money; he had a reputation for right for monetary backing, and he worked hard. Still, he was lucky. And not everyone these days is as lucky as he was.

I spent a year in Washington, D.C. working as hard as the Chinese immigrants read about in the newspaper. I would arrive early in the morning and come home late at night. I was usually too keyed-up to sleep. That's when I discovered that I really didn't enjoy what I was doing, at least not enough to be married to the job. All of my role models growing up said: work hard and you'll succeed. My father worked at the university and came home at night to run his own accounting business; my mother taught remedial reading at West Park in Ravenna and came home with migraine headaches; my grandfather worked long hours on the farm and enjoyed it. That's the difference: *enjoyment*. I can keep busy reading and writing down my thoughts and enjoy the process. Work isn't fun unless it reminds you of your sandbox in the backyard, when hours would pass by as fast as buckets would fill with sand you scooped up on sunny summer days when life was free and hours were spent in creative play. I think my cousins, my sister, the Brady's crowd, and I have the right idea about life. I think our own parents might learn from our ways: if it isn't enjoyable, why bother?

"They grow up soon enough," my grandmother used to say. My generation has learned to postpone the inevitable realism of a hard way of life. We watched the '60s generation protest against the Vietnam War, and saw four Kent State students shot to death, and still we're stuck in a rut. We don't really have power— we couldn't even stop Edward DeBartolo's shopping mall from moving into our small community. Perhaps it's too easy to give up. We have learned lessons, but still we seem as children compared to people like my grandfather who have suffered and toiled lifelong weeding celery patches and gathering maple sap. My generation has inherited that song from Todd Rundgren in which he sings, "I don't want to work. I just want to bang on the drum all day." So we're banging on our drums and will grow up soon enough. Meanwhile, life is soft.

Barn Interior, Morgan County, Ohio ©*Stephen J. Ostrander*

RICHARD HAGUE

RICHARD HAGUE is a native Ohioan, born and raised in the industrial Ohio Valley at Steubenville. He now lives with his wife and children in Cincinnati where he is the chair of the English Department at Purcell Marian High School. His poetry and creative prose writing have received awards including a 1990 National Endowment for the Humanities grant to study "Landscape and Literature." His books of poetry include *Ripening* (Ohio State University Press, 1984) and *Possible Debris* (Cleveland State University Poetry Center, 1988), and *Mill and Smoke Marrow* in the collection *A Red Shadow of Steel Mills* (Bottom Dog Press, 1991).

In this essay on the basements of our lives, Hague is both literal and figurative, revealing the deep psychic bonding to people and places. He is a master of the casual yet deeply meditative style. In his carefully detailed study, fact and truth are one.

BASEMENT

Our house in Steubenville, a 1950 vintage Ryan home, had no basement. It sat on a concrete slab smack in the middle of a narrow lot, modest, working-class, and with hardly enough headroom in its attic for the ghost of a dwarf. It was a clean house with no mysteries, no thrilling staircases to tumble head-first down, no nooks and crannies to gather the debris of the years, no subterranean dampnesses breeding waterbugs and mold. It even smelled new at first, and took several years to accumulate and ripen its own organic, individual scent. All houses have their own smell; once established, it is a permanence that lingers, dwelling like a secret under the masking fake florals of air fresheners and the bogus resins of pine-scented cleaners. It is the house's unique molecular signature, a complex mixture that blends the personal chemistry of its inhabitants with the esters and exhalations of its materials: plaster, caulk, moldings, lumber, plumbing. All of these, in turn, are compounded with the odors of the cuisine and even the pastimes of its occupants. One man who lived in my neighborhood refinished furniture as a hobby, and his house, redolent of tannic acid, smelled like an oak bog.

Children especially are aware of the odor of a place—I was, at least—and I think I might have been able to identify, even blindfolded, which of my relatives' or friends' houses I was in, simply by its smell. It is one of the special gifts of childhood, this acute sense, and I mourn the losing of it as much as anything from my youth.

My grandparents' house on Logan Street had its special smell. Their place was older than ours by a couple of generations, and its scent had matured in a time of coal furnaces, steam locomotives, and full-bore open hearths. These things it smelled of and more. When I stayed overnight there, I awoke each morning to the aroma of toast making in the broiler of grandma's gas stove. This was no run-of-the-mill toast. It was toast's zenith, the acme of bread. Beneath the alchemy of the open gas flame, those slices of Italian from DiCarlo's bakery were transformed, mixed with the varied compounds of that house's and that neighborhood's atmospheres; there has never been toast like that again. Its smell drew me from the front room upstairs, and its crusty, buttery crunch remains crisp in my memory even now.

My theory is that the proximity of the river had something to do with the quality of that toast, and with the taste and odor of the very days themselves there. Even in the clearest, most tangy weeks of late spring, the green darkness of the river two backyards away made vaguely musky the smell of the air. There existed a rich, silt-flavored micro-climate on lower Logan Street that even the buckeye in the side yard seemed to sense, sprawling widely over the sloping lawn like a fat burgher having no need to get up and exert himself.

But despite the delights of the upper reaches of the house—the middle room upstairs, which had been my uncle Paul's, and where I first read *The Adventures of Huckleberry Finn*, and the old-fashioned bathroom with its claw-footed tub and black register hoods curved like the necks of gigantic cobras—it was the house's lower regions, even below the fragrant kitchen, that most drew me in those days. For my grandparents' house had a basement, a full deep one, and it came as close as any basement I've ever known to being the archetypal Dark Place. It was at once fascinating and frightening, a tinkerer's workshop and a Merlin's secret chamber, filled with vapors and dimness.

Its door opened off the dining room. The landing at the top of the stairs was an abbreviated one, crammed with cleaning gear and rummage, and it would have been more than an even bet that a child would trip there and fall down. Even grandma herself had stumbled there and broken her arm.

But there was an additional association that raised my consideration of the basement out of the domestic and into the realm of the mythic, even the grotesque. It came in the form of a tale that no one in my family remembers hearing. Perhaps it was one of my grandfather's private and arcane concoctions, let drop of a stormy summer evening on the front porch down there by the river. It could have been. Or maybe I dreamed it, years ago, lying abed just across the river from Fairy Glen, on whose dim, timbered slopes my father and I once discovered the body of a hanged man.

Whatever, I do not resist this story's substance now, nor did I then. It has entered me as *places* often enter me, entire, in excruciating detail, though seen only momentarily, perhaps, from the corner of my eye. The slant of light over a rockface, the webbed and shattering glint of a creek through a pine grove, the silhouette of a cottonwood snag far behind, glimpsed from the stern of a turning canoe—these scenes possess me, become moments that last, images that somehow re-shape the world for me.

So has this story, which I remember happening (maybe) long ago.

Next door to my grandparents' house, her fenced yard abutting the slope the buckeye grew on, there once had lived an old woman—call her Mrs. Rainey. She was a widow who rarely came outside. When she did, it was an event the neighbors noted. Soon it became apparent to those who caught sight of her that she was suffering from some terrible ailment. On her head she commonly wore a rag, wrapped turban-like around her skull at the level of her eyebrows. Over the course of a summer, the neighbors saw that there was a kind of growth, or tumor, jutting from the top of her forehead and causing the rag to assume a bizarre, horn-like shape above her brow. This growth swelled and swelled until it was the size of a large turnip.

The women of the neighborhood were appalled. They tried to get her attention, to communicate their concern; they sent a doctor to see her, but she refused to come out from behind her half-closed door. Week by week the growth under the headrag enlarged, and the women's dread deepened to despair.

And then, one hot August afternoon, Mrs. Rainey appeared in her backyard, spryly attending her stunted hollyhocks. The headrag was tight over her brow— it fit exactly—the growth was gone.

"I was walking down to the cellar," Mrs. Rainey told someone later. "And I wasn't watching close. I bumped my head, right there where that thing was. I squashed it up against the low ceiling of the stairs, and that thing busted off, fell right in my hand. Oh, it was messy, wet with watery stuff. Well, I cleaned myself off, and I wrapped it in some old papers. Then I put it out with the trash."

Standing at the forbidden landing at the top of my grandparents' basement stairs, gazing up at the cobwebbed joists, I imagined Mrs. Rainey, and, before Grandma caught me and pulled me into the chandelier-blazed dining room, I thought I saw, in the dimness above me, a dark stain. It was peril and hope, disaster and luck. Even now, Mrs. Rainey's story continues to dwell in some limbo of my knowing, neither science nor religion, perhaps not even a "fact," but something stranger, more close to me than any of those, more chilling and more true.

Soon, I grew old enough to go to the basement on my own, gripping the banister, putting the old woman's horror out of mind as best I could. The steps leading down were wooden, and the dampness had weakened then so that they gave underfoot, sagging beneath even the small boy I was. At the bottom, a black hulk looming in darkness, stood Pap Pap's guncase, a high varnished cabinet with glass doors. Inside it, he kept two shotguns, a World War I rifle, and his fishing tackle; the smell of steel and gun oil washed from it whenever it was opened. On the wall opposite stood his work bench, an eight-foot construction of two-by-fours and plywood. Piled high on it in the back against the foundation were old biscuit tins with perfectly fitting lids embossed with *Uneeda* or *Nabisco*, and amazingly stout little cheese boxes with dadoed joints. Above, hung from the joists by their nailed lids, gleamed twenty or thirty jars of screws and washers, nuts and bolts, hinges and angle irons, casters, connectors, tiny turnbuckles, and a hundred other to-me-nameless amazements of copper and brass and iron. All had been assiduously drenched with WD-40 to keep the rust off, and so the smell of oil dominated both sides of the basement. To a railroader like my grandfather—and an Irish Catholic to boot—rust was an avatar of evil. The oil can was his holy weapon, a kind of exorcist's aspergillum.

It was at this same bench too, with its single light bulb overhead and the tiny window level with the brick sidewalk outside, that Pap Pap sharpened his knives; I remember the rhythm and silken friction of that sound: *shrop, shrop, shrop, shrop,* and I remember how the blades came from the whetstones gray and moist, and how, as he wiped them clean on his pants leg, they appeared wonderfully glinting and bright as he lay them on the bench, side by side, like slivers of razored moon.

To the left of the workbench was the coal cellar, in terms of domestic spaces now an extinct species. Too bad: the cellar and its cargo supplied an extra dimension of earthiness to the basement, and delivery days were a wonder. Delightfully frightened, I watched the great black chunks roar down the coalman's chute, and I held my hands over my ears to keep from going deaf. The cellar filled steadily, the coal pile creeping toward the door, dust billowing out into the basement. Tiny flecks of anthracite glinted in the light from the workbench window. Sneezing, I retreated to the clearer air near the bottom of the stairs, and the dust began to settle at once, a thin film on the floor. Then slamming the little steel door, the coal man would be finished. I'd run upstairs and hang over the edge of the front porch to see him drive crazily away, his truck itself a thundering confusion of rattling fenders, clashing gears, and grimy blind headlights.

Cellars within basements, darknesses within dimnesses, illuminated here and there with startling lights—like a lived-in Chinese box, my grandparents' house contained spectacle within spectacle. For opposite the coal cellar, just beyond the gun cabinet, was the fruit cellar, another night place, another set of amazements. Its door had no knob, but a carved wooden handle, slick with forty years of nervous sweat and pulling. Beyond it a frayed twine hung in the center of its darkness, a ghost string, pale and forever damp. When I pulled it, the cellar blazed suddenly before me, astonishing and garish as a sideshow. Dozens of jars of preserves lined the wooden shelves: rich raspberry-colored beets, golden peach halves, yellow innumerable nuggets of corn, the frenched greens of string beans pressing the insides of their jars to bursting. But none of their summery garden smells came through. It was aware only of the cool alien mustiness of the cellar, of the decay and bitterness of its sour earth floor, of the rotting wood, the rafters shaggy with mold and cobwebs, and of the formic smells of dead insects—crickets, waterbugs, roaches, the shiny black beetles with pincers like the horns of a stag. When I'd selected a jar of pears and clutched its coldness uncomfortably to me, I pulled the light string again; darkness swarmed up around me, and I instantly forgot all the bright fruits, the shimmering vegetables. The place closed in on me, smotheringly, and I fled, giddy with fear, into the gray light of the basement as if into the noon sun. I fastened the door behind me, pulled it shut deliberately, listening for the wooden latch to click, as if to keep locked inside it some horrid wildness. It was a wildness I already suspected lived inside me, in the cellar of myself, a place I could never completely escape, and so had to learn to live with. For consciousness was arising in those days, consciousness of the wonders of light and half-light, and as well an awareness of the strangely fertile but sometimes dangerous broodings of dark. No one could have kept me from that knowledge; no one could have— nor should have—sheltered me from its power. It was as inevitable as growth, that knowledge of the dual faces of the world, and as risky, as rewarding.

It is a telling coincidence, then, that to get anywhere in my boyhood required going down; from the ridge we lived on to town was a descent of several hundred feet, down a winding hill road my cousins from flattest Missouri were afraid of when they visited; from town to my grandparents' house was a descent almost clear to the river; and so their basement was only the logical continuation of the shape and direction my life's journeys had already begun to take. As a boy, I dug a trench and a deep hole in our backyard, covered it with some old siding from a barn, and piled earth a foot deep atop it. I sat hunkered in that darkness lit by a single piece of candle and was thrilled. During my late adolescence, in pursuit of an education, I drifted a couple of hundred miles downriver, to Cincinnati, that many more feet closer to sea level, that many more millions of years deeper in geologic time. Now, as a man, I dig down each spring and fall in my garden, turning the soil, bringing the richness—death and life combined—up for another season of growth.

And I spend time in the basement of the house we live in now, and see, among my own recent and soul-less tools, the pleasantly haunted hand-me-downs from my grandfather: his oil cans, all filled by his own hand twenty years ago, his huge pipe-wrenches, relics of his steam-engineering days. I see his tool boxes, one red, one green, like the signals of his oft-cussed but beloved railroad, still decorated with the jig-sawed letters that spell his name. I meet him in the Dark Place through these things, these old familiars, these pass keys to the house we all share. It is a reunion in silence and shadow and the earthen smells of old time.

For the basement is to me, somehow, though on a larger scale, the equivalent to that pit, "one cubit's length along and wide," that Circe instructed Odysseus to dig at the end of his journey to the Land of the Dead. After the wanderer made his sacrifices, the spirits arose, and that pit was their meeting-place, the borderland between past and present, life and death. So the basement, too, is a border, an opening midway between the lighted, busy, careering world above it, and the ancient, secret, brooding earth around and beneath it. Standing here, I am exactly at eye level with the living, root-twined surface of the earth, yet my feet are as deep as the bottom of a grave.

But it is not the end of the journey, no more than Odysseus's visit was the end of his. Both up and down exist here, both past and present, and together, they may suggest the shape that is called future. I remember, when fear or sorrow begin, how old Mrs. Rainey, that miraculous day, was going down to the Dark Place. And I remember—deliberately remind myself to remember—that she came up from it, out into the light, and that she was well.

Steelmill, Ohio Valley at Mingo Junction ©Larry Smith

LARRY SMITH

LARRY SMITH was born and raised in Mingo Junction, Ohio, and is a writer, teacher and editor. His critical biographies include *Kenneth Patchen* (1978) and *Lawrence Ferlinghetti: Poet-at-Large* (1982), and two video docudramas—*James Wright's Ohio* and *Kenneth Patchen: The Art of Engagement*. Smith's most recent books of poetry are *Inside the Garden* in *Ohio Zen: Poems* (1989) and *Steelvalley: Postcards and Letters* (1992). He is the co-managing editor of *The Heartlands Today* and teaches writing and film at Firelands College of Bowling Green State University.

The setting for "The Company of Widows" is the industrial Ohio Valley and the city of Steubenville in particular, an economically depressed area that once blazed with production from the steel mills but more recently has been forsaken by plant closings and unemployment. "This place of beauty and waste," Smith remarks, upon his return to the hometown of his youth. In a visit with his widowed mother and later at a summertime parade in downtown Steubenville, Smith comes face to face with what has changed and what has survived—"with what is here and what is not"—and begins to discover the answer to his own question: "How much does each of us give up to survive?"

THE COMPANY OF WIDOWS

Every couple of months or so I return to the industrial Ohio Valley with its deep green Appalachian walls along that big winding river. And lately as I come into town bouncing over the gaping potholes of Steubenville streets, stopping at the traffic light beside that huge bridge to West Virginia, I stare at the new monument to the steel valley, a statue of a laborer in shiny asbestos suit frozen at that moment when he taps a sample from the blast furnace floor. He seems intent upon his job, only there is no blast furnace floor, just this laborer alone in time and space. I admire the statue's simple directness, its human scale and respect for reality. For me, this whole steel valley remains as real and fluid as the hot flowing iron of memory.

As I round the curve under the Market Street Bridge, my windows down to make a summer breeze, there is that aftertaste of something burnt in the air, and I swear you can taste it too in the water, as bittersweet as rust. Heavy barges of coal and ore move down river beside me as the gray air billows from smokestacks, rises and crests in a dark heavy cloud. I am enough of an outsider now to notice this; insiders never do, or if it gets too heavy and they are forced to cough each time they speak, they blame it on the milltown across the river—"Smells like Follansbee!" This place so marked by extremes of beauty and waste, is my place, my hometown, my family—and I breathe and swallow it again.

"It ain't all bad," as they say, and I look over to see my wife awake now as we come into "Mingo Town." She smiles too at being home, and we wake our twelve year old daughter, who asks, "Are we at Grandma's yet?" I smile as the car winds up the steep hill, and pulls in before a yellow brick home. I unload our bags and leave the women here at Ann's mothers, then drive down St. Clair hill, staring into the steaming cauldrons of the mill. At Murdock Street I turn right, coast downhill, and pull in behind my mother's car. She has taken down the front maple, leafless for years, so that the whole place looks a little different and a whole lot the same; a three story wooden frame house with worn green shingles along the edge of Ohio Route 7.

Mrs. Maul nods to me as I get out—neighbors still, her yard still cared for like her retarded son who is now 33 and staring out the widow at me. I wave then note how Mom's porch needs the mill dirt squirted off. I take the broom by the door, and start dancing it across the green painted concrete till she hears me, comes to the front window laughing, "Get in here, you nut."

It is at least a five minute wait as she wrestles her door locks, three of them where once there were none. But I don't object, I want her safe, and with the recent break-ins and thefts from cars, I tell her I will install another if she wants. "Don't worry," she says hugging me home, "We old girls keep an eye out for each other."

In Mom's house one never gets further than the "television room" where the set is always on. I've found her sleeping here some nights in her reclining chair in the glow of a snowy screen. We sit and she gives me news of who has died or been arrested, and word of my lost siblings; she offers me candy and a glass of root beer. She is sixty-four this year, my father's fatal heart attack upstairs, now three years past. Though we often speak of him, of what he'd think, of how he used to work so hard, of his joking with the kids, we never address his death. We both know that he is gone—the whole house echoes his absence—but we won't recall for each other those weeks around his death when we went through his things, sorting out tools and clothes, taking papers from the mill to the social security office in Steubenville. It still breaks my heart remembering my mother sitting in that office, hearing her say to the stranger, "My husband's dead, now what do I do?"

Only this time as she brings in a plate of store-bought cookies, I am surprised to hear her say, "That day your dad died, he took a handful of these and a glass of milk. I remember, he said he was just going upstairs to lie down. He said he had to rest."

I cannot breathe for the weight of this, something caught in my own chest which somehow asks, "Mom, what happened that day Dad died? Who found him, did you?"

Our eyes just touch before she goes to sit, "Oh, yes, it was me that found him—there in our bed—asleep I thought at first, yet somehow I knew." She takes a breath as the scene begins, "He'd come home from golfing with his buddies saying that his arm was hurting. He started golfing several times a week since the mill retired him." Her eyes look distant as she talks, like she's watching all this on a television screen somewhere. "I called to him, touched his arm, and he felt cold lying there. God I was scared, so I called Darlene and she called the emergency squad. They got here quick. His friend Brownie was with them. He's the one came downstairs to tell me, 'Jeanny,' he said, 'there's nothing more we can do.' I remember him standing right here where you are, saying that. 'There's nothing more we can do,'" and she sighs. "Brownie's a good old boy, been your father's friend since they were school boys."

"Was there a doctor who came?" I have to ask.

"No, just the paramedics, but then they took him straight to the hospital where he was pronounced dead." Suddenly she looks at me as though she has awakened out of a trance and is waiting for me to explain.

Only I can't. All I can say is, "It must have been hard for you. I'm sorry I wasn't around." There is a silence between us so still that we notice the hoot and crash of the mill as the trains take a haul of slag down to the pits. The mill is always there in this town—in the sounds and smells, the color of the air and in the talk— "What they got you workin', midnight?" "We'd come up, but Michael's workin' four-to-twelve next month...." Work is the fabric of life here.

Married at eighteen, my father worked as a brakeman on the railroad at Weirton Steel for forty years, till they forced him to retire. All this is *there* inside the room—this awareness of a life.

"How'd you get through it all, Mom?"

"Well, Darlene was here, and your sister Debbie had come down by then. I think Dr. Ruksha came by and gave me something. I can't remember now. Debbie would."

There's another long silence as we think about all that's just been said. This is farther than we've ever gone into it, the gritty details of a death, and it's almost as though we've stirred up a part of ourselves we thought was dead. I smile at her, "How come we never talked about this, Mom?"

She looks back, "I don't know." And then she thinks to say, "I know he's gone—Lord how I miss that old boy—but he's still here inside this house. You know, I can feel him sometimes. I think I hear him calling up from the basement, 'Honey, where's my work clothes?' or some such thing. I almost answer him, then I stop." She smiles quietly, "I guess I'm losing touch. But you know, I always feel better when I think of him, like having him in a dream."

I go over and hug her in her chair, and we can both sense the grief in each other. "What does it all mean?" she sighs, and I just hold her, so frail and quiet.

"You did all you could, Mom. All anyone can."

Now it is I who has to move about, so I walk out into the kitchen for a drink. The radio is playing the area talk show—'Will the schools be forced to consolidate if the mills don't pay back taxes?' It's a mix of local gossip and preparing for the worst. My wife's uncle talks of retiring at forty-five. "What do I care?" he asks, "I can't let the mills decide my life. What's going to happen anyway, when it all shuts down? Have you thought of that?" And he shakes his head sitting on his front porch, "Who owns these mills? Who decides what happens here?" I shake my own head. "We steelmakers are a forgotten race." And I have no more answer for him than for my mother in the other room.

I could tell her of my own dreams of my father—of how he appeared in our house, smiling and tried to tell me a joke I couldn't get—how he laughed as if to say he was okay now. I know I felt good for a week, but dreams fade quicker than memories. Back in this valley the struggle toughens you or it breaks your heart. And where do you draw the line?

I think of how my father didn't complain of his arm or chest on the day he died, and I wonder if he might not be alive if he had. Yet, wasn't he trained here not to feel the pain, not to complain? Pouring my coffee, measuring my cream, I wonder how much we give up to survive? How much did my father?

I stir it together and know these are futile questions, yet somewhere I've learned that ignoring a truth creates another sort of pain and a kind of blind numbness around the heart. I remember how Dad, scout master of my youth, would stop our car on the street to break up a kids' fight; he couldn't let a wrong go on. His working so hard, sending two boys through college, may have been his own way of rebelling against a silent lie. I take a drink of valley coffee and sit back down on the couch.

While my mother goes to take her medication I leaf through the local *Herald Star*. When she returns I ask, "Mom, what's this parade they're having uptown in Steubenville today—a Festival Homecoming? Do you want to go?"

She smiles, "Sure, when is it?" before she can think of a reason not to go. Like a child now she welcomes small adventures and a chance for company. I know that kitchen radio is her best friend most days, that's why I bought it for her, and to quell my own guilt for moving away to my quiet home along the lake.

"They say at 2:00, but there's already a street fair on Fourth and Market if you want to take that in. Have you seen it?"

"Debbie and Michael took Robin the other night," as she sits. "They said she rode a pony in the street. I can't imagine that. Market Street used to be so busy with traffic."

"Yeah," I say, and we both know the story of how the old down town of Steubenville died four years ago after the layoffs, then the opening of the Fort Steuben Shopping Mall. Yet we both secretly wish we could be wrong about this, that the town will yet survive. Somehow our valley toughness doesn't exclude a capacity to dream.

*   *   *

At noon I show up again, having retrieved my wife and daughter. My mother-in-law Sue has joined us in this summer thirst for a celebration. A widow like

Mom, she carries her John with her all the time. Instead of wearing a widow's black, she refused to smile for a year and a half. She's a strong Italian woman whose fierce integrity and hard work make her a legend in her neighborhood. John too did his 40 years in the mills, as a millwright—humble and happy on his job till they took it from him claiming his eyes were weak. They were weak but twice as strong as the benefits the mill payed for his "early out." I know these forced retirements didn't kill our dads, but I curse the thoughtless pain they brought to good people. Sue works now in the school cafeteria—baking cookies and cakes, fish and french fries for a mob of teenagers. They give her a hard time but love her cooking. They always ask whether she cooked it before they buy...she is seventy.

My wife Ann and daughter Suzanne are like her in their strong will. In the Valley you learn early, if you learn at all, that work and self-belief are your strongest tools. My mother-in-law's favorite saying, besides "The rich get richer, and the poor get poorer" and "At least we *eat* good," is ... "Well, at least we have each other."

Ann offers the front seat to my mother, but she refuses, climbing into the back—"No, no, we belong back here. Don't we, Sue? The merry widows—and Suzanne." We all laugh, and they begin to talk as I cruise up river to the celebration, to the hope a parade brings. As we enter town from the North I search for a parking place—up close and free. I must prove to all these women that they haven't a fool for a son, husband or father.

Finally, we pull onto the hot asphalt of the city lot, and I feed dimes to the meter. We cross the light down Adams to the street fair. The parade will follow these outside streets and march a square around the intersection of Fourth and Market. It's a good thing too, as those two streets are packed with noisy citizens barking back at the game keepers, standing in line for rides, or wolfing down Italian sausage and onions with a sudsy Bud in the afternoon. The whole street smells like a local bar, and there is hardly room to pass as we bump good-naturedly into our neighbors. Aflow in this human river, pushed on, I almost lose my wife who waves a hand above the heads. We laugh on the street corner, "So many people," I say, and she adds, "And we actually know some of them," an inside joke to small-town emigrants living in anonymous suburbs where the faces seem familiar yet you know none of them.

As a rock band blasts and rumbles from the flatbed of a truck, we feel at "home." And though we know this busy downtown street will become a deserted crime area again come Monday, for a while, our memory is washed by the flood of our senses.

Sue tells Ann to tell me that it's time to find a place to watch the parade, and so I look around then lead us back from Washington, only this time along the sidewalk, past the back of the Italian and Irish booths smelling of spaghetti and corned beef with nearly matching flags, past the abandoned J.C.Penney's building, the closed furniture and clothing stores—so empty and dark inside—past the Slovak church's perogi and raffle booth, to the corner of Fourth and Adams.

The old Capital Theatre has been leveled to build a store to sell tires and auto parts. It's been gone for years, but each time it hits me with its large sense of absence. In fact I realize that I have been vibrating with this same sense of presence and absence since we arrived. Struck by the sense of what is here and what is not, I struggle to assimilate—the change.

In the midst of parents pushing their children toward a noisy, street merry-go-round, I recall how my wife and I once sat close together in the cushioned seats of the Capital Theatre while Tony and Maria sang so desperately of their love struggle in *West Side Story*. It was the first time we kissed. Perhaps my whole little family really began in search of such close moments? What I do know is that things change, even in the old town. Facing that, I know my real problem now is understanding the direction of that change.

Waiting here on the curb along the corner, I've been noticing things. Not just the noise and vacant stores but the changed sense of the place. What has survived and how? The angry fumes of the One-Hour Dry Cleaners still spill out onto the street, and I remember that sickening smell and sticky feel as I picked up a suit, standing there forced to breath it as I watched the weary movement of the women at their mangles, caught the hurried tone of the clerks. And of course the bars are still here, one for every third storefront, and the Sports & Cigar places not driven out by the legal lottery. One bakery is still open, reminding me of time spent waiting for the bus breathing the hearty bread and donut smells till I had to purchase "Just one, please" at the Downtown Bakery. All the Five and Dime stores have been converted to self-serve drugstores, the restaurants to offices or video rentals, the clothing stores empty as night.

I stand there making this mental documentary when my daughter insists, "Dad, I'm hungry." We adults suddenly look to each other and realize she is right, we have forgotten lunch. I look back to the booths, then down Adams and smile, one of the brightest moments of the day, for we are a half block away from one of the best pizza shops in Ohio, perhaps the world.

"I'll be right back," I tell them, and take my daughter's hand to lead her down the street to DiCarlo's Italian Pizza. Inside, the mixed aromas of parmesan—warm dough—spicy pepperoni and sauce bring me back. It is a Roman pizza they make, sold by the square, and the crust is crisp yet chewy with juicy chunks of tomato melting into the mozzarella cheese and pepperoni which they throw on last like scattered seed. I point this out to my child, all the while remembering those years of standing at this same counter watching the rich ritual of the men tossing dough hard on counters, of their moving the pizza up the oven drawers as it rose steadily to a climax—cut and boxed, a rubber band snapped around the corners, the holes popped to keep it crisp. We buy two dozen and hurry back to our crowd, to that first bite into the steaming slab, chewing it well, a piece at a time. And it's good to taste how some things stay the same.

Standing as we eat, I notice the need for napkins, to catch the dripping but also to keep it clean from all the street dirt blowing along the curb. "It's a shame," Sue clucks, nodding to the way litter lies along the street—not just cigarette butts, though there are plenty of those, but whole bags from Burger King, empty pop and beer cans that the residents step over, like hard stones on the sidewalk. "The city levy didn't pass," I am told, and I nod as if I understood, but it is all wrong. Like watching your child pulled from a sports game, I am really torn that what seems so precious to me feels so easily abused. Yet I check my sense of righteousness knowing how much I've moved away from here, to my suburban life, a college teaching job, a safety along Lake Erie. I do not wish to accent my estrangement. I eat my pizza silently.

People begin lining the curbs standing or seated in lawn chairs. They stand and talk or occasionally watch up the street for the start of things. The police walk by us, a kid waits then darts across the street. Something is about to begin. Watching the faces of people standing near me I look for the familiar but find only the strange...a woman in a POISON T-shirt yanking her child up by the arm—smacking her really hard on the butt, screaming "I told you to pee before we left!" This time a smack to the face, "Didn't I?" No one says anything. "Well, didn't I?" The child only wails while the mother bellows, "Now, you run home and change those pants. You'll miss the parade." The straw haired woman seems oblivious to all around her, as though the street is her home. This is something our parents and neighbors never did, no dirty laundry aired in the street.

Her husband joins her now on stage—and yes, he is a hairy guy with those dark blue tattoos flaming up and down his arms. He brushes by her. A "Hey, babe, I'm goin' for a beer!" falls off his lips like spit, as he pushes his way through the crowd.

"Oh, no you're not!" she shouts at him. "You're not leaving me again with *these kids*!" And it seems her whole life is a series of exclamations as she walks off leaving her children at our feet. They don't seem to notice, and most of the crowd looks back up the street trained now at ignoring these little unforgivable scenes of family violence. It is my mother-in-law who hisses, "Sceev-o" and folds her pizza away in her napkin. It's an Italian expression, a succinct verb that means, "It makes me sick," and I know it is not the pizza but the mean ugliness that has repulsed her. It haunts the streets as I look hard at the faces in the crowd of locals who seem as strangely foreign to me as the news from Iraq. It's like watching the films made in this area—Robert DeNiro's "The Deer Hunter," or Peter Strauss's "Heart of Steel." The setting is right but the people are all wrong—not because they are actors but because they are portraying the valley and its people at their most desperate to preach Hollywood despair or false hope. That film life feels close yet alien to anyone who knows this place, a twin hurt that confuses me like these wounded faces around me. They are not the faces I grew up with who lived well here though poor, and shared the good that they had and were.

As I watch this woman turn back I try to guess her age, but it is impossible—the facial lines and glassy eyes, yet her young children at our feet. She turns to us, motions to her kids, yells to my puzzled mother, "I'll be right back!" And so we find ourselves baby-sitting her girls on the street corner. They take no notice until we offer them a pizza which they take and gobble down, thanking us only with their eyes. It's an awkward scene, but this human gesture seems the only way to dispel the curse of this family's life.

"Who are these people, Mom?" I hear myself asking.

"Oh, I don't know her," she says, then realizes what I've asked. "There's a new crowd that lives here now."

"Where did they come from?"

Sue answers, "When everyone started moving out of downtown, they started moving in." She gestures broadly to the old buildings across the street, and I see above the storefronts the backs of buildings—windows with ragged curtains, bags of trash out in the street beside junked cars. And my heart sags like the dirty clouds or this child's heavy diaper.

"Apartments are cheap now, cause nobody wants to live where so many muggings go on." Sue goes on to report the worst and most recent incidents while I wonder which came first—the crime or the abandonment. She can't help telling these stories, because it has happened to her friends; it's a part of her life now. She plays out her old storyteller's hand—hoping in telling it to somehow understand.

And I think of another conversation last week with a city planner now working as a car salesman. "No jobs for city planners," he jokes. So when I tell him of my dismay at understanding the way cities change, he describes for me the 'myth of urban renewal.' "See, they throw up a few new office buildings that look good to the outsiders. Right?" I remember nodding. "Only what you don't see is also what you get. To the city poor it means something else—less and worse housing. Where do you think all the 'homeless' people come from?" He asks while downing a half cup of coffee. "I'll tell you. Urban renewal drives some of them into the street and it drives a lot of others away—to smaller cities like your hometown where they have no sense of past and no hope of a future. And so there they live *unconnected*, just using up the present."

I had nothing more to say then nor now, as this parade begins. I just stand here thinking: of the fathers who worked this valley farming labor into families along the river land, and of the widows now forced to watch the rich soil used up, spoiled by greed and unconcern. I know that my father had no answer for this, and for once I am glad he doesn't have to be here to watch it all happen. I just stare across the street at an older man tending cars in the parking lot. He moves aimlessly from car to car, checking tags, and I recognize something in his face. My mother whispers his name—a classmate of mine wounded in Viet Nam. I know his face as a shadow of my own.

Held there on the curb of the Steubenville street that feels so close yet strange, I know how little there is to say. And as the parade goes by, I watch how the faces light up at so little. The children are smiling at a clown squirting water from his motorcycle. A float of Junior Women toss candy at our feet. I smile along with our mothers. Yet inside myself I am thinking of the five words given to me by my ex-city planner: "Abandonment creates its own culture." It sums up my own confused pain now, and I say it over and over to myself, "Abandonment creates its own culture." In the summer heat the parade passes, and then we take the widows home.

Conkle's Hollow State Nature Preserve ©Stephen J. Ostrander

LAURA SMITH

LAURA SMITH is an Ohio native now living and working in Portland, Oregon. She has worked as a journalist and cafe waitress and poet. She has served as an editor for Portland's *Rain City Review* and for Ohio's Bottom Dog Press. Still in her twenties, she has lived in Bar Harbor, Maine; Boulder, Colorado; and Portland, and travelled to Italy and Taiwan.

Beginning in the here and now of her life, she connects with a family memory, them weaves the story of her Hungarian grandfather, her Italian grandmother, and her own long, hard bond with them and her Ohio life.

HARD ROOTS

Woke up this morning feeling as if I'd dragged my voice for miles and wrestled with it in my sleep. I put on a white ribbed undershirt, one of those thin tank tops that cling softly and cottonly to the dolphin skin of the torso, and I looked down at my stomach and saw my grandfather who used to slowly swagger his Hungarian barrel-body down the hardwood hallway, past white shiny walls and framed prints of The Madonna & Son hung like square windows into a dark, thick world of saintly sorrow and haloed serenity. My grandfather, in these episodes of my memory is donned in pale blue boxer shorts and the same kind of thin white undershirt I had on. His pink shoulders roll into plump biceps out from the white, clean cotton.

His crew cut hair was the same white and the only place that cropped fine manicured lawn of dove down, that I remember touching on him. My mother rubbed his head too, let the ends of the upright hairs sweep her down-turned palm. He sat beneath the hand gulping a swallow of his highball, resting his knuckles on the kitchen table, fingers holding a fan of blue and white patterned playing cards.

Rubbing his head so, we knew that he was good, that his heart knew love and that he had found the freedom within the repetition of his hard labor days which those Christian deities of his walls, those icons of the laborers who knew suffering, held before them. Those little paintings brought home from church or sent through the mail showed clean and rosy people who radiated light into dark brown backgrounds that could have been Ohio Valley hillsides dusted with coal, lined with tall smoke stacks and railroad tracks.

My mother said to me years after Grandpa died that he never hurried, that he wasn't ever itchy to go somewhere other than where he was, that he would sit his largeness with the rest of us and never be the one to talk of moving along to the next thing.

My grandmother turns into a woman when she tells us about his clean body walking up the Church Hill every day until he dies. He walked alone, homeward from the store, from church, for where the bus dropped him after work. He always showered thoroughly, Grandma tells us, at the mill before coming home in the early evening for dinner, a ritual of small dignity that rendered his Eastern European fair skin holy. She straightens her back and lowers her voice a little when she tells about his tenderness, about seeing him look out from the window in the days of his retirement, holding the curtain back until he saw her walking home from work, and of how he'd have coffee brewing for her when she walked in the door. She even tells us that no one can touch her like he could and how she misses it.

He died when I was a quiet eleven and he was seventy-something. It was the passage of a brute labor era, the one in which America had been erected by the hard-pumping vigor of small people who shoveled and scrubbed and bled. He held the hard stories inside himself. There's only one picture I know of from his past. It's of his parents, fresh from Hungary, robed in heavy black wool, staring with hurt and contempt into the camera. Deep lines carve the outline of his mother's stony jowls. His father's shoulders are square.

But my grandfather seemed to have stepped out from under the iron shovel of his father's fisted hand: he could laugh. He just drank his highballs at home in the kitchen with his strong Italian wife telling stories while she rolled meatballs and stirred the sauce.

He had heart attacks before both of his daughters' weddings, scaring everyone with the heaviness and silence of his ...worry? concern? sadness? of his life? He died of a heart attack finally, sitting in his eye doctor's mechanical vinyl chair. His youngest daughter, a nurse, straddled him and tried, and failed, to resuscitate. The ambulance came.

My mother heard the news from my father when he burst quickly and seriously through the door carrying an armload of books and freshman compositions home from work. He reached her in two wide steps, gripped her shoulders firmly, and said, "Your father's gone," loudly and hard. I was curled on the chair next to them, able to look up and see my father's sad paleness and my mother's shoulders' sudden slouch. I ran dizzily to my room. How could my mother and I have been laughing together while at the same time my father had been driving home full of this death? I was wishing the drive had taken longer.

Now, I, who have been held in the arms of the proverbial proletariat, am a freckle-faced woman who waits tables in a poets' cafe. I see my own body as living fruit of generations of hard labor and good food, and I watch West Coast bohemians talk about restlessness in bitter monologues. I sit by this pond in the park in my white undershirt wanting to work hard and swallow a highball in the evening, wanting a barrel-body and a good wife, wanting to hold stories tightly inside myself and use them to touch the ripple on the pond left by the skimming breeze.

Bigelow Prairie Cemetery, Madison County ©Becky Linhardt

PHIL BOIARSKI

Author, poet and essayist PHIL BOIARSKI was born in an area overlooking the Ohio River in Eastern Ohio. To date, he has had three books published: *Short Love Poems*, Silk Screen Press; *Coal & Ice*, Yellow Pages Press; and *Cornered*, Logan Elm Press. His work has appeared in *The Paris Review*, *The Rocky Mountain Review*, *The California Quarterly*, *Ohio Journal* and *The Minnesota Review*. In addition, he is the recipient of numerous awards and honors that include Ohio Council for the Humanities and the Arts Grant, Southern Classic Poetry Prize and COPA Award. He is a member of the editorial board for *The Kid's Connection Magazine* and is a member of the board of directors for Days of Creation Arts Program for kids, an organization he founded. Boiarski lives in Galloway, Ohio.

"A Figure in a Moonscape" is set in the outdoors in the Ohio Valley, an area so desolated by strip mining that it has come to resemble a moonscape. With gun in hand, Boiarski takes you back to this scarred place, where he blasted woodchucks and devoured a library's worth of books as a teenager. In "A Figure in a Moonscape," Boiarski creates a sense of place that is at once idyllic and foreboding, familiar and surreal.

A FIGURE IN A MOONSCAPE

I was born overlooking the Ohio River and raised around Harrison and Jefferson Counties, on Foxes' Bottom Road, about eight miles outside of a very small town. Most evenings, you might hear one car roll down the road all night long. Our house was in high hills like those that trail for twenty miles or so on either side of the river. James Wright was from Martins Ferry and Bill Mazeroski from Tiltonsville, but everyone in the Ohio Valley, all along the right side and bottom of the state, knew what they came from, a steel mill and coal mine culture that plundered the land and employed the average Joe whose kids left as soon as they could go.

I played football, first for St. Casimir's in Adena, Ohio, then for Adena High School, which had a short-lived glory as the Golden Wave, before being absorbed with all its life-long rivals into Buckeye Local Consolidated High School.

When I drive home through the hills of Harrison County, I see what progress has wrought on the landscape of my youth. Many of the mines are mined out. Much of what goes on is coal processing and delivery. The shining tracks of coal trains and backwoods pipelines pumping a slurry of crushed coal to Ohio utilities crisscross the land like ivy vines. Now the lakes and reclaimed streams are tourist attractions. In my childhood, reclamation was not a consideration. I can still take you to places that are like a moonscape, surreal in their desolation. Then, this land was less populated, and signs of man were fewer and further between.

It was not uncommon for me to walk for an hour in these hills and not see another house. When I was in high school, I often took my .22, a book, a sandwich and canteen and disappeared into the wilds for the whole day. The land would go from pasture to strip pit to hardwood forest, to the mountains of the moon, and the closest thing I'd come to seeing another human being was an empty *Iron City* bottle or the dark red and brass artifact of an empty shotgun shell.

But mine was a forest for the trees mindset, the most obvious sign of human beings being omnipresent gaping wounds in the earth, the strip pits themselves. Strip mines are signs of human activity, but more absences than presences, miniature Grand Canyons where the "overburden" has been lifted up (Hallelujah!) from the valuable bituminous beneath, and left a certain nothingness. Usually, after a decade or two, a pit fills with a blue-green water that brings birds and field mice and woodchucks. I spent the better part of six summers slaughtering woodchucks around the landscape of surface mines. Some places I knew not to go. My cousin Mike drowned in the quicksand of a spoil bank. One guy I knew was attacked by a pack of wild dogs and fought them off with his .22. I felt safe with my weapon, or at least, safer.

Being young and armed, I imagined myself an Indian, an explorer, a soldier, a scout. I climbed the hills and slipped silently down into the valleys. If I saw humans, they did not see me. I left no sign and took no liberties with myself. Since I didn't shoot his cattle or harass his other stock, Mr. Dombrowski encouraged me to hunt "chucks" or groundhogs. They were hard on his farm equipment, destructive to his crops, and created holes his animals broke legs in. I saw them as rodents and, like mosquitoes, not really one of God's better ideas.

Of course, the groundhog was just an excuse to have a gun. Mine was a Remington Nylon Sixty-six, a sort of survival rifle, made with a green polyethylene stock with parts of nylon and steel. A semi-automatic, it weighed a little over three pounds, even with an eight power scope, and held fifteen long rifle, hollow point cartridges in its magazine. It made me feel like I could hide out in the hills and hold off wild dogs or Russians all by myself.

I wasn't crazy or careless, though. We had a neighbor with an automatic Mauser who would shoot at anything that moved, including trees that swayed a little too much for him. He had a tree behind his house, a full foot in diameter, that he had blasted in half over a week's time. I prided myself on being a careful hunter and a safety conscious person. I had the discipline of fantasy and often stalked a groundhog for hours, watching a group feed and sun itself before waddling down to the water a few at a time to drink. I would wait and read my book. One summer it was science fiction; another it was *The Brothers Karamazov* and *Wuthering Heights*. I read every book in our small town public library. *War and Peace* came the summer of my senior year, most of its incredible pageantry played out in the barren spoil banks. Between chapters, while Pierre and Natasha were moved about like miniatures in a giant diorama, I rid the world of what I thought were vermin in massive battle panoramas of my own.

To make it easier, I gave the ones I killed names like Stalin, Molotov, Beria. The ones that got away I called Tolstoy or Pushkin. When they were relaxed and unsuspecting; when the fattest, oldest male, Old Joe, himself, his harem having assured him the coast was clear, sauntered down to the green water pooled in the old strip pit to sip; I would line up the cross hairs in my scope, and carefully, holding my breath in anticipation, squeeze off my first shot. After that, I didn't waste time watching him fall, but slipped into a fervid, almost maniacal frenzy of rapid fire aiming and shooting. Focusing fast on the rodents closest to the hole, I eased off shot after shot, before they could scramble madly back into the earth. I had spotted and noted them all, and had watched where their alternative entrances were. I ran off all fifteen shots, then fell silent and reloaded.

I would repeat this process, a time or two in the space of an afternoon, at different places in the wildest part of the hills. I once single-handedly wiped out a colony in a summer of steady visits. They had set up in a particularly barren area that resembled a lunar landscape. Not a tree stood beyond the escarpment of the spoil bank. Not a bush sprouted, nor even very many weeds. In the distance, a road wound through the rubble up a hill to a graveyard with a few big old oaks. This place had not sold its mineral rights and stood like the core of an eaten apple on an empty table. Except for this island, it looked as if a bomb had hit and blasted away all the vegetation down to the dirt. From my hide, behind a few rocks, I could watch the groundhogs, and hidden in the shadows of a place where the coal company had not touched, separate myself and my world from those rat-like lives. Ending one of those lives seemed easy for me then.

Other than woodchucks, I wasn't much of a hunter. My brother hunted squirrel, rabbit and even deer, but I could never get too involved in killing anything even remotely cute. The closest I ever came was a raccoon that was raiding our chicken coop when I lived on a commune. I carry the karma of a few hundred groundhogs and one thieving raccoon. I wonder how I'll have to settle up in the next life. And I wonder about my other rodent victims, the muskrats.

I did some trapping with my brother around that time, mostly muskrats. We went out together before first light to run a hundred trap line, but he made most of the money. He actually had the ability to skin the corpses, a part of the process I was willing to bargain away ninety percent of the profit just to avoid. We both set the traps in the holes, at the entrances on the banks and under the water. We both staked down the chains so they couldn't drag the trap away. He killed all the rats that were not dead already with a Louisville Slugger. I suppose I was an accessory to those killings as well, since I helped. One of them had almost gnawed off a leg when we sent him out of the park. Several achieved success with this grotesque method of escape. We even caught one with only one front paw.

Once, we fought a mink who had decided that he had found this muskrat corpse first, and had certain property rights. A mink is actually an animal that borders on cute. It looks exactly like a little mink stole, except it will not sit still like a stole, so it's hard to get a good look at one. It moves very fast in any and every direction at once, and hitting it is akin to trying to connect with a hummingbird. This particular mink was not cute in any way. It jumped all over the both of us, delivering such quick and vicious bites as to draw blood in a dozen places in less than ten seconds. It sprang from one to the other in a blur of fur while my brother alternatively cracked himself or me with the ball bat. Not once did he actually connect with the mink. When we came home, ripped and bleeding and black and blue from the battle, it looked as if we had been attacked by a lion at least. My mother laughed all the while she patched us up.

But muskrats were part of my winter, just as groundhogs were part of my summer. I lived a life woven into the seasons like the seamless threads of fine cloth. As soon as the ground thawed, I helped plant onions, walking a plank between the rows to keep a true line. After the planting, there was gathering. My seasons were identified by their gifts: morels, puffballs, wild asparagus, and in the summer, strawberries, raspberries, blackberries. The fall was the time of apples, pears and pumpkins, like edible icons of time's passing. Everything gathered was eaten or preserved for the winter, a meaningful and almost magical connection to the movement of time.

Across from our house was Dombrowski's farm, where I worked for fifty cents an hour baling hay, picking strawberries or feeding cattle. I could not hit the neighbor's house with a rock if I threw it as hard as I could. I could yell at the top of my lungs and he couldn't hear me. I suppose it was this openness, wide enough to let the yell dissipate to a whisper by the time it got there, that influenced my way of looking at the world. I see myself now, looking back on those years, as a figure in a landscape something like an enormous old quilt. Patches of it are lovely and almost richer than reality. Other squares are tattered, ripped open, moth-eaten. Others are simply holes in the shape of a space. Some seem eerily like the surface of the moon. Only a few years later, when Neil Armstrong, from Wapakoneta, stepped off the ladder into the desolate dust "for all mankind," he could have shot that video in Harrison County.

I've always felt the openness, the forest's intimacy, the expansive moonscapes and meadows, all the relative emptiness of this place, was a wonderful accident of my youth. It wasn't always pretty, and it often was lonely, but it was never dirty and crowded. I have since come to live near the city with neighbors close enough to hear in the summer when the windows are open. You learn to accept house after house and car after car. But you can never get the same feeling about raspberries or pumpkins, magically exploding out of the ground, increasing exponentially like an expanding universe, when all you have is a grocery store to connect them to.

Once, when I was about six, my Uncle John took me out looking for morels. These tawny, delicate creatures hid their delicious presence deep in the woods on steep hillsides in the shade and shadow. I had eaten them several times and found the flavor wonderful, at once nutty and meat-like, the essence of spring. We searched in places he alone knew and it was hard work. He was a big man, overweight and red-faced. He always seemed to be straining, grunting, breathing hard. We climbed steep grades holding roots to pull ourselves up. When we found some of our quarry, we would kneel like pirates who had found gold and laugh out loud with uncontained delight. It was a treasure hunt and we were getting rich.

After we had visited all his secret spots, he took a circuitous trail back. We stopped in a pine wood and he showed me a Boletus, so beautiful and normal looking, you might think it was a perfect mushroom. He took it in his hands and broke the cap. On contact with the air, it turned a deep indigo color. "The blue is a sure sign of poison," he said.

Over those years, I became familiar with the process of strip mining. I even worked for the coal company while earning my way through college. I was assigned to a foreman who put me where I was needed. I might be a flagman directing huge trucks over dirt roads. I might sweep up the shop or drive a flatbed from one site to another. The strangest job I had was with a pump crew for the largest earth mover in the world. It worked day and night to rearrange the land in an upside down fashion. "The spoil," as it was called, was what was left when the machines moved on. A huge mountain of debris was heaped next to a pit, the other side of which was a sheer cliff where the vein petered out. The cliff itself is called a spoil bank, and it truly is "spoiled."

The Gem of Egypt was the name of this monstrous piece of equipment. It stood as tall as an eight-story building among all the ill-assorted end-dumps and front-loaders, drag-lines and drills that swarmed about it like an army of mechanical accomplices. And dwarfed to the size of ants, men swarmed around it, moving cables, operating equipment and pumping water. I ran hoses thick as my thigh from the rapidly filling hole over the nearest hillside. Portable pumps that had to be started like lawn mowers sucked the discolored water away from the tracks and cables. I worked and watched while a whole hill disappeared into piles of unrecognizable tailings.

And coal, black as hematite, shining jet-slick in the sun, was loaded on the backs of enormous Euclid trucks with twelve-cylinder Cummins diesel engines so loud most of the drivers gradually went deaf. It was an awesome display of Man conquering Nature. More or less. Many times after the "bull gang" had moved the huge pieces of equipment away and the land had been left alone, the acids and ores in the soil would leach out into the streams and turn them orange and useless. Fish would gasp and die. Muskrats and groundhogs would flee, if they could, and what was left was a fetid, useless wasteland, the spoils. I could show you places.

I suppose the men who did this had a rationalization of their own in mind. I don't know if it was Russians they were fighting by raping the earth. Who knows, who knows. Perhaps, like me, they needed the money for a good purpose, and what the earth gave, mushrooms or minerals, was theirs to take. Whatever their reason, I was an accomplice and that too is part of my karma, like the cute woodchucks I blasted like some mad assassin. I haven't used my rifle since I went to Ohio State.

It was November, my freshman year. I was walking across the oval and started to notice people crying. Women, at first; then I noticed men, too. I walked past a knot of students with a radio and the voice of the newsman came to me in snatches. I reached the dorm and got to my floor, where I ran into a friend. He was crying, and asked me if I had heard.

"Heard what?"

"The President," he said. "He's been shot in the head. He's dead."

Fox farmhouse in southern Ohio ©*Robert Fox*

ROBERT FOX

Originally from Brooklyn, New York, since the mid-1960's ROBERT FOX has adopted Ohio as his place sense. After some shifting (which he documents here) he and his wife settled on a farm in southeastern Ohio where he also taught at Ohio University. More recently they and their two children have migrated to Columbus, Ohio, where he serves as the Literature Coordinator for the Ohio Arts Council.

In addition to writing stories, poems, and novels, Fox is an accomplished blues guitar and piano player. Among his book credits are *Destiny News* (stories, 1977), and *TLAR & CODPOL* (*The Last American Revolution* and *Confessions of a Dead Politician*, two novels, 1987). His work has also appeared in *Sudden Fiction, Three Genres, Best Ohio Fiction*, and *From the Heartlands* (where you will find the sequel to this essay). His fiction has earned him the Nelson Algren Award for Short Fiction and the PEN Syndicated Fiction Award. He also directs publication of Carpenter Press and is currently completing an audio tape of his music and a book of nonfiction about his migration from Brooklyn to Ohio.

This personal essay recalls several times and places as the author and his wife began their young life together, moving from Brooklyn, New York, to Carpenter, Ohio, to Levittown, Pennsylvania, and finally back to southeastern Ohio and the farm not taken, and the one that was. In a casual tone he sketches in the details of a time in a life, capturing a vivid remembrance of an American era and a personal connection to place. It is a tale of relocation.

THE FARM NOT TAKEN

Two roads diverged in a yellow wood,
And sorry I could not travel both...

-Robert Frost

The year in Carpenter, near Athens, Ohio, was a good one, despite the area's notoriety as "Hippie Holler." A herd of wild ponies lived in the wooded ravine behind our house. Just before thunderstorms you could hear them whinny and clatter as they rounded each other up to find shelter. They were once mining ponies, turned loose when the mines closed. Mrs. Howery, who ran the once prosperous grocery on State Route 143, stocked her former store and the old hardware with hay. In winter, she fed the hay out over the barbed wire fence.

A single White Rose gas pump stood in front of her door, and when the supplier remembered, she sold gas in amounts ranging from fifty cents to two dollars. Hers was a self-service pump before those became popular, but she stepped outside in her bonnet to unlock and then lock the pump. Our neighbors around the bend on the county road were an assortment of artist-intellectuals, marijuana growers, local farmers and city-bred homesteaders. I raised my first garden behind the house, using warm compost to grow green peas, green peppers, green onions. I grinned like the gardeners in the seed catalogs, astonished and proudly sharing my first produce.

A year later, when we found ourself in a slab home in Levittown, PA, we knew it was only temporary. The few tomatoes planted by our predecessors there were stolen upon ripening. As we moved in, neighborhood kids peered into our living room through the glass walls and later announced that according to their parents we must be hippies. Why else wouldn't we have a television? "What do you do at night?" one of the little spies asked us. We hung up bedsheets until we acquired curtains.

Though Susan and I came from Brooklyn, three years in southeast Ohio gave us a desire to continue country living. I accepted a teaching job in New Jersey harboring a pre-turnpike image of The Garden State. During the search for land that ended somewhere between Vineland and Glasboro, we stumbled upon Arneytown. It was an unpopulated version of Carpenter. We could not easily learn who owned the one decaying house and overgrown fields that had potential, and a further search wasn't worthwhile for it was too far from Lawrenceville. So we compromised with a rental in the Pinewood section of Levittown, PA. (All the street names in Pinewood begin with P--we were around the corner from Poets Lane, the shortest street in the section.) Unlike the apartments we contacted, pets and children were welcome. There was some land for our coonhound Traveler to roam, the huge yard of the Walt Disney Elementary School, with a blown up sepia halftone of Mickey Mouse in the lobby--the screen dots large as golfballs.

Some mornings the air was pungent with the odor of molten plastic or the heavy rotten-egg smell of hydrogen sulfide. Levittown was flanked by Monsanto, 3-M, and the Fairless Hills U.S. Steel plant. Motor vehicle exhaust from U.S. Highway 1 and State Route 13 added to the airy soup. My journey to and from Lawrenceville where I taught included a traffic circle glittering daily with the debris of fender benders. I survived the circle, but did get rear-ended leaving Princeton one evening.

When I rejected a teaching contract for the following year, my chairman asked, "And what are you going to write about in Ohio, cows and pigs?" In his view I was holding our for a raise. (He thought I had taken the teaching job to be closer to New York City, since that's where I'm from.)

And did I realize, too, that I was abandoning the security of a teaching career? Somehow I could not view the fragmented and alienated lifestyle of that part of the country as security. Susan and I agreed that where and how we lived was more important than career. I was not brought up to take such risks, but as the oddball in my family, it was simply a matter of course.

Once, while hitching home from the Volvo dealer on Route 1, I was offered a ride by a young man who, like me, had grown up in Brooklyn. When I asked what he thought of Levittown, he blurted out ecstatically, "Man, this is country livin'!" Shortly before we left, a neighbor asked how we liked living there. We described southeast Ohio and, wanting to be polite, said we were slowly adjusting. She confided that she had arrived from a farm in the Poconos ten years earlier and still had not adjusted.

After an aborted attempt to move our glassware back to Ohio in a Citroen whose rusted hydraulic system burst in downtown Baltimore, we loaded a U-Haul truck, and with the Volvo in tow, Traveler behind the wheel, drove back to where most of our friends lived, determined to buy an inexpensive piece of land where we could garden and raise sheep for wool and meat, and where Traveler could roam without being accosted by angry neighbors waving wooden coat hangers.

It took some doing to persuade Ward and Joan to rent us the old house on her home place. The new cinderblock building with the picture window facing the road was their rental property and it was occupied. The old house was drafty, heated by two space heaters which might not be adequate...but we described our ultimate aim and they welcomed us.

There are a lot of township and country roads in southeast Ohio called "Sand Ridge" and "Sand Rock Road," named after the ever eroding sandstone. Our Sand Rock Road was a ridge north of Amesville (formerly Mudsock, home of the Coonskin Library, Ohio's first). The ridge was high above Leading Creek, but more than once we had to take the high road home through the scenic town of New England.

I set up my writing desk on the landing of the second floor looking out over the tops of Macintosh apple trees at the distant blue hills in the northwest. It was a rapturous view, one whose meditative stillness would have kept me from writing had I not disciplined myself to ignore it and continue expressing my tumultuous psyche.

Ward pastured cows on the ridge,and in winter, if I was home evenings, I'd ride out with him on his 8N Ford tractor with a portable plastic windshield and a load of hay on the lift. We talked about raising cows, sheep, putting up hay. Ward showed me around the huge barn whose foundation was dug into the side of the hill. "Grandpa" had kept livestock in the basement area, whose outer walls were whitewashed sandstone. It was partitioned with stanchions for calves at one end, and mangers for lambing at the other.

Listening to Ward's stories, I pictured myself waking to the alarm every few hours on February mornings prepared to help warm, steaming lambs into the world. I imagined what it would be like loading hay in the mows above. I pictured the long narrow chicken house bustling with clucking hens, imagined the feel of warm eggs in the nests at dusk.

It was all in reach and I was ready to get to work. With the bow saw and hatchet I used for camping I pruned dead wood off the apple trees, cut down and sawed up a barkless elm at the edge of the garden, and stored the wood in the coal shed. We thought of installing a wood cookstove as well as using wood for backup when moisture froze in the regulators and cut off the supply of gas.

Even in the sunless part of winter a surprising beauty came to the ridge. Fog rose up from the bottoms erasing the land below. Looking out beyond the silo and barn we appeared to be an island nestled on a cloud. Only the constant ticking of the gas pumps connected us to the reality of the invisible world.

Two friends had recently purchased thirty acre farms for five thousand dollars. Our goal was to find a similar homestead. The land on our side of the road, which contained the buildings, came to almost thirty acres. Two hundred and twenty acres remained across the road. If Ward and Joan would sell, we thought we could afford our side, though it would be more expensive than what we initially sought. Ward and Joan consulted their sons, neither of whom wanted the home place, and offered to sell us the entire farm.

Fifty thousand dollars--though ten times more than our initial goal--was reasonable, Ward insisted. He totalled the royalties from the oil and gas wells, the income from the cinderblock rental, and then said that the timber alone would pay for the place. "I...I couldn't cut any of it," I said in my uninformed conservationist innocence. "I don't mean clearcut," Ward explained patiently. "Just take out the ripe timber. Be a waste not to harvest it. Gives the young trees light and room to grow. Then, in a few years, if you need a tractor or a new truck, you'll have some more to cut. And by the time you have kids ready for college, you'll be all set."

It was promising but overwhelming. My parents never bought anything they couldn't pay cash for, which meant they never had a car. My only major purchase up to that time was the Volvo, which took our entire savings. The house alone needed structural as well as cosmetic work. And as to farming, apart from feeding fallen apples to Molly and Betsy, the Holstein and Guernsey in Ward's herd, I had no experience with livestock, had never driven a tractor, didn't know the difference between three-point hitch and drag type machinery.

"Nothing you can't handle," Ward said, encouraged by my ability to adjust the valves on the exotic looking Volvo and the housewiring course I took at the joint vocational school. But I had more than second thoughts. From my perspective, how could I portion my time to balance outdoor work with and intellectual and literary life? It didn't seem possible.

One day in early spring Ward and Joan took us around the property. As we started out, Joan pointed to the green '56 Ford sitting in the driveway of the corncrib on its original whitewalls. "That year, after the hay was in the barn, the corn picked and the wheat threshed, Dad decided he needed a new car. He went to Athens and wrote a check to Mr. Beasley and drove the car home. You know, he made more money out here than men in town with good jobs."

We passed the cinderblock house which was occupied by a university student and his wife. Almost every day throughout the winter, the young man's .22 cracked in the woods. A pile of squirrel pelts was stacked near the back door. By spring, we heard that his wife threatened to leave if she had to fix squirrel stew once more for supper.

Behind the house, the land sloped gently down to the woods. The trees were tall and straight, the ground spongy with decaying leaves. It was the clean floor of old woods, some crackling deadfall but no underbrush. Ward stopped to indicate white and red oak, beech and tulip poplar. He linked his palms around trunks to show us the minimum diameter that should be harvested. He pointed out large beech trees with rotted centers that would make excellent firewood. "It's easy to pull a trailer around in here, not like most of the hills in these parts where you'd need a team of oxen."

We came to the creek Susan and I visited on our walks. We referred to the site as the Salem commercial and thought of it as an ideal picnic location.

"Dad would eat dinner here," Joan said. "When he was working on the hill, he'd come down to the shade with his lunch pail and set on one of these rocks."

"I'll bet he drank that water, too," I said.

Ward and Joan smiled. "Cows pastured upstream," she said. "But there's a spring yonder where he refilled his jug."

As we continued up the hill I ran my hand through the abundance of orange broom sage, also known as sedge grass. Ward explained that it was a sign of acid soil, easily killed by lime and fertilizer. He described the hills green with clover and alfalfa, wheat barley, the pasture dotted with sheep and white-faced cattle when Grandpa farmed it. He admitted he was making it sound easy but he knew we weren't afraid of hard work. Except for our lack of farming experience we were like them. One winter they had dug out a basement under their first home by hand.

We crested the hill and came to an abandoned house. Susan and I never had come this way in our wandering. It had been a sturdy frame structure, but the large sandstone foundation blocks now looked like anthills. The sills at one end were mired in the earth. Ward opened the door. The hardwood floors remained intact. We entered. Black, white and marbled porcelain knobs were still attached to the cherrywood doors of the different rooms. Wallpaper, though faded, still hung intact on the downstairs walls. We climbed the almost vertical, tilting stairs to three small, eaved rooms where I found a copy of *The Farmer's Guide* in good shape. The back cover was a full page ad for a Maxwell automobile. I opened it and handed Ward an article on the benefits of green manure.

"Their crops grew, let me tell you," Ward said. "Now my dad didn't buy into the chemical fertilizers the ag men started pushing in the '20's. They told him it was a work saver and to think of the leisure he'd have. He said he wouldn't know what to do with all that time!"

We stepped outside again and stood by what had been the front porch. Susan asked why someone would build a house so far from the roads, especially back then. "Road used to run right in front there," Joan said, pointing to a level path fifty yards downhill. "You can see the wagon tracks in the way the grass grows." Indeed, you could. "Mail used to come right through here. Further up towards

New England is what's left of another home, a spring house is all that stands now. The main house was struck by lightning and burnt down years ago."

"There was a one room school up there, too," Ward said. "All that's left is some old folks' memories."

"I like this house," I said, studying the weathered clapboard curling away from diagonal sheathing that covered the plaster and lath. I wish it wasn't so far gone."

"It's not all that's gone," Ward said.

I looked at him to explain.

"It's a way of life, too. They cut the timber and planed the lumber for that house right here. Set up a sawmill in the yard. That's the way they put up buildings back then. Everyone pitched in. As recent as Grandpa's time there was no such thing as a job in town and farming on the side. You depended on your farm and relied on your neighbors."

"How old do you think this house is?" I asked.

Ward studied the siding, the exposed sheathing, pulled a few loose nails from the wall and handed them to me. They were not the round nails I was familiar with but flat-sided, like railroad spikes. "These are early factory nails," he said. "They go back to before the Civil War. Wouldn't you say?" he asked Joan. She shrugged her shoulders.

As we headed back Ward returned *The Farmer's Guide*. "This may be worth something someday."

"I don't think collectors would be interested," I said.

"I'm talking some time in the future," Ward said, "for your kids. If you all do settle on a farm, it may mean something to them when they're grown."

"That's real thoughtful of you," Susan said.

"Talking to you folks has brought back a lot of good memories," Joan said.

Ward agreed. "Anymore life changes so quickly you can't remember what you've forgotten. Wouldn't you say?"

We separated on the way back to the creek. Ward and Joan talked to each other intently and we thought they were ready to name a price for the hilly, wedge-shaped piece of land we lived on. We were familiar with current property values and hoped their offer matched our guess.

They joined us and we continued walking together. Ward spoke up. "We'd really like for you folks to have this whole place," he said. "Our boys won't have it, you know, but it would still be like keeping it in the family if you bought it. Now I know you think it's more than you can afford and that it's too much farm. We know you've never farmed and all that. But we'd help you get started. We mean it. And the boys would help out, too. We know it. You'd do just fine. Wouldn't you say?" he asked Joan.

"We've seen a lot of young people come and go through here," she said. Lots of nice young people, too, but not the kind to settle down and make a place like this home."

We crossed the creek on the stepping stones and entered the woods. "It's just so much more than we think we can afford," I said.

"You'll get it back in rent, royalties, and timber, like I said. That's all money right back in your pocket."

"I know," I said to Ward. "But it's mind boggling. I think maybe we should just continue renting for another year or two, save some more money."

The word "rent" agitated Ward. "I tell my boys, 'Rent for as short a time as you possibly can. Put your money towards something you'll own, can trade.' That rent, it's just throwing money away on something you'll never own. Like I told you, we'll give back your rent money, right off the selling price."

As I looked up, the sky seemed to change color through the budding treetops. An oak leaf from last fall drifted towards me. I wished it was a check for the down payment. I'd sign it right then, pass it over, shake hands.

Susan and I, in the meantime, looked at other farms but found nothing to bid on. We planned to stay on Sand Rock Road. I took a sheep shearing course from the county extension service. Ward spread several loads of manure on the garden and was about to plow it when a farm we had seen before moving to Levittown came up for sale, on the other side of Athens in Dog Holler. Before driving to see it again, I found a four-leaf clover in our yard. As we talked to the sellers, I found another.

Were these signs? Was each choice a good one? We were the first callers on the farm. The people who followed us were disappointed.

As happy as we were with our unexpected find, we knew we had let down Ward and Joan. Apart from whatever disappointment they may have felt, they were glad we had found a place we could be comfortable with. When they visited us after the move, they could see why we bought the place. The house, the outbuildings, and the combination of hayfield and pasture on seventy-three acres seemed just right, they agreed. Although we were completely broke once again, we had almost everything we needed to start farming, for I bought the tractor and equipment that was on the place. The former owner of the machinery lived up the road, but I doubted there would be neighbors like Ward and Joan to advise us. Ward assured me there were many old farmers around only too happy to pass on what they knew, but that he and Joan were just a phone call away.

Not long after we moved to Dog Holler, a tornado touched down on Sand Rock Road. It blew down the 150-year-old white oak tree in our former front yard, tore the roof off the corncrib, and twirled the plum trees by the kitchen door out by the roots. A timber company from New York state bought the entire farm for ten thousand more than Ward and Joan asked of us. They harvested only the ripe timber, sold the old house and wedge-shaped land we lived on to a young couple from Athens at the price we were willing to pay, and rented the cinderblock house to a pair of young men from Amesville. One night that fall, in 1973, a recently returned Viet Vet from Amesville drove up to the rental house and shot his friends dead through the picture window as they watched TV. Hearing the shooting, the young man in our former house went out with his .22 to investigate. He took a .9 mm slug in the jaw but fired back. The vet managed to drive back to Amesville where he died in his car.

Would these event have happened if we lived there? The tornado would surely have struck regardless of ownership, but would we have rented to those ill-fated men from Amesville, or more likely to someone in the university community? Had we rented to those young men, would I have ventured out unarmed (I didn't own a gun.) to investigate the shootings, or would I have immediately called the sheriff? Would I have become a successful farmer on Sand Rock Road, prospering on oil royalties after weathering the first Arab oil embargo? Or, would I have realized much sooner that the kind of conscientious commitment to the land I wanted to make (farming in a traditional, labor intensive way without chemicals) was full time and unyielding?

At some point in our deliberations I consulted the *I Ching*, with some misgivings over a materialistic motive. All I retain from that consultation is an image of moving clouds and water, and a storm that would pass.

Perhaps it told me that some choices are as good as others. Perhaps that farm could have turned me into a successful (not necessarily prosperous) farmer. It also could have chased me off the land discouraged and in debt. Or, I could have persevered there as I did in Dog Holler until another major choice had to be made.

Wild mustard near Nelsonville ©*Stephen J. Ostrander*

GAILE GALLATIN

GAILE GALLATIN lives in Zanesville and is a professor of art at Muskingum College. Her poetry and essays have been included in anthologies including the *Writers Against War* collection done in Iowa City. In addition to her painting, painting which is often of Ohio landscapes, she is a violinist in the Mansfield Symphony Orchestra.

Perspective is what is offered here as she brings her fresh Iowa eyes to this Southeastern Ohio landscape. People and land are bonded in a remarkable sense of place which she captures as well in her art. It is her habit of journal writing—of listening and seeing and recording—that gives this piece its easy form and intimate voice.

NEW TO THIS STRETCH OF THE ROAD

Like the slight inclines that roll couples towards the center of a too-soft bed, the hills of Southeastern Ohio have conspired to tumble us towards each other; I rolled and bobbled in from the west, roller coasting the long definite inclines that mark the end of the post-glacial area of our Midwest, and you tumbling sparkling in from the east by way perhaps of the Cumberland Gap. Leaving Iowa, I drove on straight highways that tore past billowing fields of corn, of beans, and groups of buildings or rows of trees which edged the boundaries of the fields. There is a moiré effect in passing rows of corn, a palpable energy in the slight hills which shares the taut surface of a trampoline: Iowa land is energy about to emerge. Your route from a rural area in the East brought you up and through the Cumberland Gap, tumbling down into the hills of Southeastern Ohio to settle a new space.

Our friends were waiting in the ravines and cliffs near the place where Clark Gable was born, or grew up, or both (I forget why and how much Cadiz is claiming him), and there are other friends too, strolling over or coming by or flying in. One brought his family from Iowa, only later than I, and met me his first night in the village when he talked with the priest who stabled his donkey in the basement of the house I was renting. The donkey should have been hitched to a tree in the side yard. Quite early the next morning, the priest led his donkey to Old National Road and continued his trek to a shrine in Mexico. My friend decided to stay, and he and his family found an old farm house with a grand porch looking out over a slight dropping-away of land that would be called a hill where I grew up, but not here.

Our little bed is quite full now. If this land were a comforter, and we could all grab hold of the edges and pull out all the folds and gathers, and unbunch the bunched up places: the area would be considerably larger. We would then see each other across a larger expanse of land, see each other clearly, full figure, head to toe. As it is, we catch sight of each other, a glimpse of a friend, perhaps only a sense of his legs as he climbs the porch steps while I drive towards the house, perhaps a whole person for a short space of time before the next hill rolls up and hides him, perhaps visible again around the next corner of the path.

Rolling down into the center of the basin between the ridges, it is rather hard to find each other: maps are written and rewritten, plans made, unmade, remade, reconstructed, abandoned. People follow each other places in cars, and again follow others home, deciding to leave when someone who knows the way is ready to head home.

Heading to a new home, the Conestoga wagons which crossed this area of Ohio, waving over the S bridges, braking reluctantly as they descended a hill, probably protesting as they went up the next, seem like portable versions of our permanent land ship: rounded sides holding what is valuable; tilting, leaning, inclining in directions that have no relation to geometry. Our land is made up of basins surrounded by ridges, a basin of large and less large hills, a basin in the center of ridge roads, a concave area which collects fog, fog which is persistent, faithful, which nudges most mornings from sleep.

Yes, we are all travelling along here, in these hills, along these roads; paved roads, gravel roads, disappearing and dwindling-out-to-nothing roads. Driving east, I see houses and barns tilted against the sun, the high horizon all curved and slanted, with hills, trees, and buildings piled up on each other. Roads start from these buildings, I can see that, and soon I see a place to turn: Hidden Drive is what is marked. I think that most people here live on Hidden Drive, that it and Ridge Road pretty much cover the territory. This particular Hidden Drive pitches up beside what I call the real road, which is timorous and tentative anyway, to Iowa eyes, and bends on up, curving and disappearing towards those buildings I noticed. This all happens quickly, even though I cannot muster the 45 miles per hour speed limit that frustrates some local drivers. Do the two roads meet? Or is it one road seen twice? Perhaps there are two roads, seen by ends only.

Foliage and worn buildings soften the curves of the hills, the twists and spins of the path. Radio waves soften and bend to get here, to arrive in the country from the village. Radio reception leaves something to be desired; that something usually clarity and fixed sound. That static used to bother me so much I would not be able to listen: now I hear through it. Perhaps those from here do not realize how easy it is to communicate—by phone, radio, or other waves—outside of these wave-catching hills. Our telephone connections are precarious, our radio sporadic, the TV sparkles and changes. Even the printed news comes out in uneven bursts of ink, some faded and pale like a shy cousin standing in the corner waiting for pie, some blurred with too much eagerness, like that cousin's pugnacious little sister, one thumb and index finger pinching the pie crust, her eye on the back of the aproned cooks, careful.

I hear through the static on the car radio; I see through the fog which refuses to lift, which remains in the basin as I drive towards the Ridge Road, on surfaces sudden and various: gravel, pounded earth, and, finally, pavement. Glancing at the map, I turn after the pink farmhouse towards the fallen down barn that used to hold a Mail Pouch tobacco sign, and see the horses in the field. A good sign. It is good weather, so most of our friends will be able to arrive on time. Everything stops, or should, in the event of inclement weather. Salt is our method here of ice control, and salt is a tentative cousin indeed.

Imagine that we do all get together on or near that grand porch looking out over green grass, bushes, and some small trees; well, not everybody, because Rita has a wedding to attend, and John went back to the dulcimer shop, and Kate and David have decided to take clogging lessons again, but this time from the other teacher. Part of this particular evening could belong in any time I remember from the earliest days. Sitting on the top porch step with my eyes closed I hear Carla say, "I was always backward as a child." I know now that this means "shy"; it is all right to say things like this, and in this case it refers to the reason Carla would not go alone to the market. After two guests manage to fix the commode (I know from my grandmother what this means), we discuss the new barn, built to replace the one that burned. The Amish came to build the new barn. Barn raising methods here have not changed: I believe my great-grandfather would have understood the process I observed in Southeastern Ohio, even though he lived in Greene County, Missouri, in the 1870s. We start supper. Talk. Sing. Leave-taking is quiet, slowed by the dark. Those of us left on the porch watch for the little red lights of the cars dipping down round the curve and, gone.

Dark again. The friends gathered here, and those absent from this supper, remind me of the workers in the old glass factories which flourished here in the first half of this century, workers who would use up the molten glass at the end of their day by making fanciful forms of all different colors. These shapes are called whimsies. A whimsey is what was spun into frivolous, extravagant shapes; a red and clear glass slipper, tiny; an iridescent and marvelously useless glass walking stick. Whimsey.

That is what we are doing here: taking the remainder of our day's work, and using it up in delight, in frivolous whimsey, in a lopsided, uneven, wobbly, and rollicking delight. I believe that some local inhabitants huddle beneath this quilt of a land, insisting on their need to ignore the present. I believe also that others of us, those friends laughing and telling tales, those companions catching sight of each other in this partial crumpled up broken pushed together, gathered-up land, that we see this land, this region, this landscape, and we profit from it.

Like kids hopping on a feather bed, like cousins rushing out from the farm yard to welcome the city cousins running in from the wagon; we are playing here, seeing here, loving it here. The best part of here. We are all tossed together in this Conestoga double bed of a valley, driving over rolling hills to visit with each other and with earth, with nature, and we are nature, part of nature.

When I first came to the village, which holds a mile or less of the second version of old Route 40, someone pointed to three trees east of town and on the west side of Old National Road. "George Washington surveyed here, using those trees," he said. At the time I thought it was embellished local color: this would have happened a long time ago, and besides, the trees were not very big. But now I am beginning to take this as fact; to believe absolutely that this information has carried through, remaining in the hills, sticking to the ground, not swayed by new roads or persistent fog: something that happened. And people still tell it. And, once past the static and fog, the loss of easy full vision of friends, the missing of other places, it is possible to see our home here, and to observe enough roundness, enough hills, for every purpose, for everyone.

So I take walks on these hills, follow gravel paths to see deer, and am refreshed by the continually changing views of the land which surrounds me. I tuck my own comforter around me at night, listening to the moon, the same moon I know, the moon that shines on my own land, to the west.

Madison County Barn ©Becky Linhardt

DOUG SWIFT

DOUG SWIFT lives outside of New Concord, Ohio, where he teaches English at Muskingum College. He has done writing residencies at Yaddo and the Virginia Center for Creative Arts. Born and raised in Connecticut, after short stints as a construction laborer, gas pumper and worker in a helicopter factory, he attended the University of Bridgeport to study poetry and filmmaking. His graduate training in writing came from the University of Iowa Writers' Workshop and the Johns Hopkins Writing Seminars. His poems have appeared widely.

The author is working through his own life here by asking questions. In fact, the inquiry mode is what gives this essay its rich detail and honest lucidity. We feel the writer getting closer to life, his and our own.

IN MY SOLITUDE

Billie Holiday croons on the stereo. The candles—still burning—sputter black clouds from the last wax in their brass holders. Food remains on the two plates. A forgotten beret lies on my coffee table. Outside, a car whines in reverse; headlights retreat, distend, sweep away, as the crackling driveway yields to pavement. With a forward hum she is gone. Another relationship is ending before it has begun.

***

"I want something to happen for you," a married friend says. She means, I believe, she wants me to meet someone, a friend; to marry, have a family.

Families, to me, are exotic—like cities I can visit, but never live in, with customs I can learn but never take to heart. I recently weaseled my way into one family: we had dinner at least once a week; held hands for the dinner prayer song ("Look around and you will see/ A family community,/ We are brothers, sisters all"). I changed Ian's diapers, twice; took Anya to COSI in Columbus. I came over for three Thanksgivings, and even slept over one Christmas Eve, woken in the morning by two stealthy children. I rediscovered the pleasure of mindless compulsive game-playing, dealing out "one more hand" of Skip-bo into the yawning hours of the evening. The comfort of families is merely in the being— a respite from my new relationships, where divulging is all. Secrets are revealed at your own risk, in families. Once out, they may be used against you when the next argument unleashes. But if you don't tell, no one will ask. This was the great appeal for me. They knew nothing about my own pitiful relationships, my hopelessly hopeful (in a haunting, taunting, memories-of-days-gone-by sort of way) attempts to try again, and again.

When I suddenly realized what folly I had undertaken in one case, when I backed away before even mere lust could be satisfied, and when I failed to even remotely fulfill her honest expectation that I explain what was wrong (which elicited her retort: "You're a mess." Amen), I crawled to my adoptive family that night, listened to the parents bicker about bills, heard Anya's sorrow because her Daddy yells too much, watched Ian romp, bellow and bawl, scooped out butter pecan ice cream, sprawled on the floor together, sharing afghans and pillows, to watch *The Neverending Story*. And it was good.

But they moved away. I had no rights to that decision, of course. Now other families invite me for holidays, and never ask certain questions, and I color and play and make up stories with the children; but I know for sure that I am visiting a foreign land. I am not making the dark passage through blood to family. Not yet.

***

I live alone on thirteen acres down the southerly slope of Zane Trace Ridge, in a replication of a Williamsburg colonial house. The anachronism suits me— I love that emotional state of *beginningness*, the spare human pitted against the wild continent, a history of oppression nipping at the heels. By poignant juxtaposition, my colonial house sits one and one-half miles south of the National Road, freeway to the western frontier, and one-quarter mile south of Zane Trace, one of the oldest roads in Ohio—still rutted in mud and gravel. On certain days, when the oil derrick down Union Way is stilled, and no plane has begun its long descent to Port Columbus, I can feel the wilderness about me, the texture of meadowlark and bluebird song, red-tailed hawks shrieking, the pileated wood-pecker hammering fiercely.

And I feel the storms, here, as I never did while living in town. When they whip in from the west all the birds hunker down. The winds smash my wide brick fireplace. I, inside, alone, can feel every rattle of glass, shudder of house frame, smatter of tin chimney hood. If alone. The first weekend I lived here some friends came over for dinner. While we ate, a storm with tornado potential gushed through, but the human chattering and nattering, small talk and tales of catastro-phe, screened out the storm. After dessert we stepped outside to watch the crisp cold front sweep the sky a deep duck-blue as the meadow of goldenrod glowed, and a double rainbow arched over the shrinking shards of lightning to the east. Somehow, I felt I had missed the elemental drama.

But alone, attuned to each intensifying gust, listening for shingles shorn from roof, screen door slammed open, house rattled on its frame, the body becomes a fragile thing. The horse and cows out my kitchen window face the storm, lower their heads into it. So I learn to face it, the terror, as rain throbs the windows on either side of me and the bricks shudder in their mortar. I feel my arms yearn to hold on to someone, friends and old lovers flashing through my mind like lightning, the terror tightening as each disappears. Spasms of sobs burst from my gut as thunder and lightening—smashing in sync above my house—thump the earth. And then. Reprieves separate the flash and crack. The rain draws tender. The sand of walnut trees stills. The house gallops friskily in the first breaths of crisp northern air. The stars prick and sew up a looming blackness, and this slope of land turns from the last node of sun, slips under a quilting of stars. My sleep that night is sound, my dream images crisp. I stand at a furthest point of land. Stars and astral bodies glimmer and swarm and fall down to an ocean that offers up its own luminous bodies, swishing and swarmed. Now, standing at that thin piece of land between ocean and starlight, stands the body of a woman, populated as a continent.

I have never known whether to be warmed or chilled by the beauty of this image.

***

I moved out to the country to write. I've learned again the old lesson that writing must be transitive, it must take on objects. As I "read" the experiences of my years out here, flipping through my journals, I am surprised by what else I learn. My nifty little house amounts to little. I suddenly see there, not writerly solitude, but emptiness. I see in the garden—a garden that flourished with broccoli, lettuce, beets, brussels sprouts, dill, and more that September I took the place over from my landlords—that this spring promises nothing. I have not worked the soil, and it feels like a kind of sin. I had come out here to lay my sorrow upon the landscape, offer it to the winds, the rains, the violent days and the calm. I had sought to practice the Rilke injunction:

Don't be afraid to suffer, replace
the heaviness back on the earth's own weight:
the mountains are heavy, so are the seas.

You couldn't support even the trees
you planted as children, they've grown so great.
Ah, but the breezes...ah, but the spaces...

Ah, it takes a tree to feel the breezes and spaces. To feel life's sorrow, you must plant yourself in life.

***

I love the wild spaces outside the city gates. Several nights ago, before attending a cocktail party for a "single" philosophy candidate (I'm always asked to meet "single" candidates, and it is in regard to this event that my friend has wished that something will "happen for you"), I was lured by a full moon to a driveway that descends from suburbia through spruce forest, to the gravel reservoir road. I recently saw two great horned owls mating in those pines—their broad wings unfurling darkness; their deep, soft but thrumming *who-who-who's* stirring the bones. I pass the fallowed field wherein I watched six deer leaping away under a previous full moon. The reservoir is frozen. The ice dulls and silvers the moon's reflection. I see the silhouette of a sparrow's nest in some bare brambles, and I hear the righteous whining of Canada geese on the other shore, shaded by beech and birch stands. The geese are close, but I cannot see them as the pitch of their squawking rises, fretters, screams, then succumbs to rippling calm. There is drama at the water, and I feel grateful that there are no humans around to dispel it with chatter.

"You aren't committed to people," the parents in my adopted family used to tell me. Keith added, "You're committed to other things, and there's nothing wrong with that." Kris shook her head. They knew, they knew that even when I was in the living room with Ian weaseled into my arms, or upstairs putting glow-in-the-dark stars on Anya's ceiling, or reading her *In The Night Kitchen*, that I was an outsider, not one of them. And I'm afraid it's true. Inside the gates, family justice prevails: someone will yell at another simply because ego is out of whack, or life becomes sad. It feels labyrinthine to me, the disappointments and guilt. Who left open the window and let all the flies in? Who broke the brown mug? Whose turn is it to wash the dishes, put the kids to bed, take out the garbage? (Why aren't you who you used to be?)

I retreat to the indifferent dark, back to the sparrow's frozen nest, back to where the Canada geese thrash and squawk. Only out here can I feel for the real injustices, our inherent spiritual poverties—without futilely blaming the closest (dearest) human being for them. "We have only half a loaf," says the stepmother in "Hansel and Gretel," "and when that is gone all love shall be at an end."

***

The candles sputter out, stench the acrid air. I leave the dishes unwashed, go out for a walk along lightless, muddy Union, up to the Zane Trace Ridge where I can gaze out for thirty miles to the Coshocton smokestacks. I wonder at all the little galaxies of family, all the lamplights glimmering. I recall the domestic violence cases regularly reported on Ohio Public Radio; I recall those of my students who are in a perpetual flinch from living in such homes. I counterpoise the families who are—miracle of miracles—by and large good to each other. Who care for one another despite the muddle, the infinite slights and cuts of speech; who stay their angered hands until they can offer a glass of soda, or take away an emptied plate. And if I enviously wish, sometimes, that I could live inside the gates and play this role, I have seen in the eyes of some of my married friends the wish to take my role, to be looking in from outside, to be free of it all. I pray for them to get over it (dear Lord above): I am no more free than they; they are no more trapped than I. And I have a powerful and curious need for them to survive whole in the lamplight. As, perhaps, when glancing at a darkened window excited by wind, they may feel a need for me to survive, out here, whole.

Rural Appalachia c. 1940 ©Tina Brian

DANNY FULKS

DANNY FULKS was born in Guyan Township, Gallia County, Ohio, near the river village of Crown City. Since 1968, he has been on the faculty at Marshall University in Huntington, West Virginia, where he has taught classes in the English honors program and school of education. He is the author of four books in the field of education. His articles on Appalachian social history with an emphasis on his native southern Ohio have appeared in selected journals including *Goldenseal,* and in *Timeline,* a pictorial journal published by the Ohio Historical Society. Currently, he is compiling a book of Appalachian stories to be published by Bottom Dog Press in 1995. He resides in Huntington, West Virginia.

Danny Fulks' powerful depictions of the lives and mores of people in southern Ohio's rural communities work through detail. One of the relatively few authors writing about Appalachian Ohio, Fulks is almost anthropological in his approach. "Big Meeting" reveals the essentials of people's lives through their apparently inconsequential objects and actions. Fulks selects and uses telling details that subtly recreate not just the events but the mood of a past time and place. In "Big Meeting," he makes rural, working-class folk who lived in southern Ohio in the early forties live again.

BIG MEETING

They came down the dirt road that ran along Greasy Ridge and the roads that snaked along the rich bottom land in the Indian Guyan valley. Some came in cars, rusted out Plymouths and Chevrolets, and old Model A Fords churning up dust that settled on the ironweeds and daisies that grew along the ditches. Farmhands with sun darkened skin and sinewy muscles bummed free rides on the running boards of the landowners' cars, holding on with one arm stuck through the open car windows and wrapped around the center post. Some came walking, groups of scrubbed boys and girls laughing and giggling, the younger kids running on ahead climbing over and under fences, skipping rocks across the green water that stood in pools in the creek bed. All roads and trails led to the white frame church that sat on the high knoll by the graveyard. This was Good Hope Baptist Church in Gallia County, Ohio. It was 1940.

The lonesome sound of a thousand June bugs rang out from the grove across the valley on that hot August night. The church bellkeeper, a hunchback man dressed in bib overalls, paced up and down the gravel-covered church parking lot, chainsmoking Camel cigarettes, a habit he picked up in Uncle Sam's Army in World War I. One by one, the people stepped through the church door and made their way up the aisles and sat down on the homemade wooden benches. The pale yellow light from six coal oil lamps that hung along the walls flickered on the scene. Millers, fat from their summer feeding, buzzed on and off the lamps. As eight o'clock approached, a new black LaSalle coupe with an unspoiled layer of dust clinging to its shiny chrome and paint crunched through the gravel and stopped near the church door. The preacher, Clifford Cremeans, had arrived.

Cremeans was a man of the Lord. Dressed in an off-white linen suit, he stepped from his car and walked into the church. His body movements and square jaw exuded authority and respect, even from the drinkers and brawlers of the community. No one looked this man in the eye that didn't look away first. He owned the night. And as he walked up the aisle to take a special chair up front beside the pulpit, the congregation, believers down front, sinners in the back, stood and sang:

> Standing on the promises of Christ my King,
> Through eternal ages let His praises ring,
> Glory in the highest, I will shout and sing,
> Standing on the promises of God.

Many did. In these hollows where coal banks spilled sulfur into the creeks and hillside flats had to be grubbed out for a few rows of tobacco, there really wasn't much else to believe in. A doctor practiced two miles away at Crown City, but his knowledge was fairly primitive. Roosevelt's New Deal had brought electric power through, but few had the money to buy a full complement of appliances. Everyone except the undertaker and a few merchants used outdoor toilets. Most young women married early and bore as many children as nature allowed. Fewer babies died than in the great influenza epidemic of 1918, but still they died. Down and out people were either taken in by families or they went to the poorhouse.

Most people had never traveled beyond local towns like Gallipolis and Ironton, let alone Columbus or Cincinnati. A few adventurous men did, however, join the Civilian Conservation Corps and wound up clearing roads in Nevada. Blacks, Catholics, and other human types were out there somewhere, but seldom seen and never understood. The only people who had gone beyond high school were schoolteachers, and they were locals who had gone off for a few semesters and returned with the same values they left with. There was some hope in fellowship and brotherhood, but this was based on following the Lord and keeping His Commandments. There was no middle ground. One group was saved for eternity by coming forward, repenting, being baptized, joining church and staying out of trouble. The rest were lost. Old enough to know better, they drank, blackguarded, worked on Sunday, stole chickens, fought and fornicated. A major task for the saved was to bring this group into the fold.

Most people came to the big meeting because they really believed there was a better world "over yonder" and only those who followed Jesus and lived right would ever see it. These included mothers who prayed and asked others to join them in asking the Lord to rescue sons who had grown up without receiving Christ and so were lost. A few quiet skeptics came as their ancestors had for a hundred years—in the tradition. The youngest ones came because their parents made them and there wasn't much else to do except listen to Jack Benny on the radio or chase lightning bugs in the summer night. And there were those in their teenage years who came to meet friends, to be with other boys and girls, to flirt, perhaps make dates for future nights as the meetings continued. It wasn't unusual for a few shotgun weddings to take place in the springtime following these revivals. But all those who came had one thing in common—they were a part of a community of human life struggling for existence and truth. The true believers would pray aloud in a united prayer and voices unspoiled by the wands of choir directors sang:

> Just over in the glory land,
> I'll join the happy angel's band.
> Just over in the glory land;
> Just over in the glory land,
> There with the mighty host I'll stand,
> Just over in the glory land.

Inside the church the air of dog days hung close to the floor. Old women fanned their faces with complimentary hand fans provided by the local undertaker. The varnished oak altar bench, lately polished, sat in front of the pulpit ready to accommodate any sinners who could be induced to come forward near the close of the service. An upright piano in the front corner rang softly with minor riffs at the hands of a teenage girl in a summer dress. Hardwood benches nearly filled with people stretched from the front of the church to the back. On the wall high behind the pulpit, a framed reprint of an unknown artist's conception of Jesus of Nazareth, the popular Jesus with a bearded white face, looked down upon the stark accoutrements and plain people. Near the picture a mahogany wall announcement board revealed that the previous Sunday School attendance had been 48 and that $16.48 had been collected in love offerings. And as the girl at the piano sounded a mighty chord in 4/4 time, once again the simple music of country faith came forth:

> Where He leads me I will follow,
> Where He leads me I will follow,
> Where He leads me I will follow,
> I'll go with Him, with Him, all the way.

Preacher Cremeans took over the service from a lay leader, put on his glasses, and quietly read several verses from the Bible. Then he closed the book and began to speak without notes, strictly from his own persona, as they say, wherever the spirit moved him. He removed his jacket and threw it to the side, men and women near him shouting, "Amen, amen." He walked back and forth behind the pulpit calling out, "Hey, how many of you love the Lord, huh; how many of you know you're going to heaven when you die, huh; you know this could be your last day on earth, huh?" The sweat came and he wiped his face with a white handkerchief. He told them how his life once belonged to the Devil. How he used to guzzle beer in the Gallipolis beer joints, get into fist fights, and pick up fast women for the night. But the Lord with His grace had saved him from all that. Since the night of his conversion he not only quit those worldly sins, he didn't even have lustful desires anymore. Praise God. He continued, slower now and looking for eye contact with sinners sitting in the back rows. He told them of a dream he had had many times. He sat in the shade of a huge maple tree that stood near the creek bank where the water was still and deep. It was deep summer and a breeze from honeysuckles and bluebells swirled gently about. All of his loved ones were there: His mother holding a covered dish of potato salad. His father sitting on the running board of a Model T Ford. His brothers, sisters, aunts, uncles, and cousins talking and laughing gaily. But when he awoke, many of them were gone. Long since dead and lying in graves dug in the poor dirt of Guyan Township. He paused. There was no sound. He stepped down from behind the pulpit standing closer to his people and mesmerized the true believers with words, gestures and tears.

The eyes of the faithful stayed on the preacher. The women continued to fan and the men removed their wool suit jackets. Babies who had cried off and on, even one or two who had been slapped by their mothers, were stretched out asleep between adults and older brothers and sisters on the bench seats. A few hardened sinners eased out of the seats and out the door, every remaining head turning to see who was leaving. And after nearly an hour of intense preaching, his voice and energy exhausted, the preacher extended the altar call and the crescendo of emotion wilted as the crowd stood and sang:

> Oh, why not tonight?
> Oh, why not tonight?
> Wilt thou be saved?
> Then why not tonight?

As the soft, sweet singing continued, Cremeans begged the sinners in the back rows to come forward and seek forgiveness for their sins. He asked them to seek salvation, to come and pray at the altar. Kind old women with buns in their hair went back to personally beg each sinner to come forward. One woman told a reluctant man in his late twenties that his dead mother was in heaven and he would never see her unless he was saved. He told her to get the hell away from him and ran out the door. And the woman understood: The Devil had ahold of that man. Another young man left his comfortable seat in the back corner and made his way forward slowly up the center aisle. When he reached the pulpit area, he sank to his knees and placed his head on his folded arms on the altar bench. The singing stopped and the preacher joined other true believers in loud praying for the man's soul, asking the Lord to bring him through. They prayed, loud and long in choral tones rising from their knees one by one as their voices gradually became still. Then the young man, his eyes wet with emotion, pushed himself to his feet and stood facing the others. The preacher and the church members fell in line passing by to shake his hand, offer congratulations, and, sometimes, to embrace him. And as the line moved forward, everyone now shaking hands with everyone else, they sang that ancient piece which transcends all cultures:

> Amazing Grace, how sweet the sound,
> That saved a wretch like me!
> I once was lost, but now am found,
> Was blind, but now I see.

In groups of threes and fours, they headed toward the rear of the church gathering together in families and groups much as they had come. They visited leisurely with friends and acquaintances as they left the church, going outside into the sultry night air. Many who had walked took rides home in cars. Most would be back tomorrow night, even though the men faced a ten-hour day in the yellow tobacco fields and the women must peel and cook peaches for canning. The sinners would even come back, although they knew they would once again face the preacher's chastisement. This was, one must remember, the last great get-together in that area until the fall, when Mercerville School would sponsor a pie supper or a Halloween carnival. As the preacher eased the big, white steering wheel on his LaSalle to the left and passed out of everyone's sight, he pushed in the cigarette lighter and shook a fresh Lucky Strike from its crisp, green package. Walter Winchell was ending his radio newscast warning of a big war across the waters. But here on Indian Guyan Greek, the September rain would soon end the sludge of dog days and, who knew, maybe a dozen new converts would be candidates for baptizing.

Conkle's Hollow State Preserve ©*Stephen J. Ostrander*

BRIAN RICHARDS

BRIAN RICHARDS was born in Columbus, then moved through grade school at Gambier, high school at Perrysburg, then college in Bowling Green. After stays in New England, California, and the Pacific Northwest, he returned home to Ohio, settling in the state's rural southern region, where this essay is set. Here he has established his Bloody Twin Press as one of the fine letterpresses publishing in the Midwest. His own books of poetry include *Loose Fish* (in *Blackbook* 1977) and *Early Elegies* (1992).

"Tucker's Run" uses a loose, journal form to record with vivid detail a way of life in Ohio's hill region to the far south. In so doing, it documents the writer's own sense of self in place. Richards asserts strong values of individualism and community, which he finds compatible in his native grounds.

TUCKER'S RUN

A Buckeye, I, born in Columbus on the Hilltop, second and third grades in Gambier, then Perrysburg until college at Bowling Green. I headed to Massachusetts for grad school and thought never to live in the Midwest again, seduced in turn by the culture of New England, the novelty of California, and the arcadian beauty of the Pacific Northwest. Then back to the Berkshires to start a family on land that had grown too expensive to buy, when my brother and I learned that my aunt was selling my dead uncle's homestead in the Ohio River Valley. I paid four hundred dollars for my share, five acres of hickory hillside cut on the north side by an intermittent run named for my uncle's grandfather, who settled there directly after he mustered out of the Civil War. The first cabin I built sat on a hillside in the deep woods above the one spot flat enough to be the garden, looking east along Tucker's Run and across the small valley to the ridge on the other side of Upper Twin Creek.

Five years later Mikki and I separated and I went to live with Dawn, exiled to a lost holler named Mackletree for the sycamores that line the stream. It was ten years before we got back here. The cabin became the print shop, and Dawn and I built the house we live in now at the north edge of the garden backed up against Tucker's Run and looking south across the Ohio to the steep ridge beyond the Kentucky shore.

***

I have developed the same respect for the marketplace that I have for a drunk with a loaded gun: an implacable desire to get away. Though I've been everything from a logger to a nude model, it is still difficult to find useful work in hard times. They call it poverty. You meet a better class of people here. There are a lot of intelligent people working in the system, easy to talk to, easy to respect. I'm glad they keep it spinning. But, as Shriner Sock said to the stretcher, "Not me, not on that." I'd rather be a monk, but I don't need an abbot to check up on me, and I don't like waking up alone.

***

Carrying Pee Wee's foal down to Dick's upper barn like a cross between a baby giraffe and an Airedale with the hair on its face still wet, Pee Wee charging around trying to knock me into the chicken yard. Then I had to fight with her to see who was going to get into the stall with it.

A few hours later I was putting a headlight in the truck when Nancy ran up to tell me that Dick's barn was on fire. I thought of the foal but she said the lower barn, so I yelled for Hal and took off. Ronny was throwing hay out, and Dick was backing the tractor in to save the baler. I grabbed the tongue, and Ronny threw the pin. We ran outside as the fire drafted along the walls thirty-five feet to the roof behind us. We turned and saw the baler frozen to the ground and the tractor wheels slipping. Ronny jumped to pull the pin, but Dick yelled "I'm on fire!" and we abandoned it all and took off for the pond with flames shooting out over our heads.

***

Pruning the last of the vines at the winery, warm sun on a cool day. Heavy breeze along the river, phoebes small in the trees on the bank, red-tailed hawk over the hill. Across the river, what looks like a toy crane dumps coal into a toy train. It takes a couple of seconds for the toy sound to reach my ears. I can stand doing the same job every year, but not every day. Seasons going around the sun.

***

The people daily closest to me insist they can't tell what I mean by what I say. I preserve that ambiguity in my poems, though I found it there. Nobody knows what it means when it is full. An overflowing cup can't be measured, though the adjective describes it. The more you can take, the more you get took.

Too afraid to love, too afraid of being criticized, shutting others off, too afraid of being shut off, too afraid of not finding a place to be alone. Being alone.

Thrushes, their twittering shaky nervous voices filling the garden and ready to mate. Yellow petals on the cinquefoil. Jack-in-the-pulpit treasured not for its scarcity, but for its reticence.

In my confidence I insist on my own way. If I don't get it, I withdraw. My totem is the hog-nose snake, or any other wild creature spitting defiance, backing away, cat who walks by himself, showy orchis behind the post pile, red baneberry. So much of the world unknown, polyphemous moth Lily pointed out in the driveway, wings torn with rain, on the desk all day, curtains tapping on the window, twenty-three eggs like millet. You'll get what you want if it takes forever. Where do I get off? but where I am shown the exit.

***

The condo avium. Tanager mating dance: fandango in the garden followed by waltzing in front of the bandstand maple off the front porch. Mr. and Mrs. Thrush from the beech tree above the well hopping around helping themselves to chick starter and a little sand from the box. Female scarlet tanager on a hickory branch, perched for a full minute with her tail high in the air before he appeared nervously light on both sides of her, then on top. The briefest of ecstasies.

***

The open window frames a darkness almost imagined, gray vertical at right center, the undersides of dogwood leaves barely green in the kerosene lamplight unable to penetrate the deep woods night. Tree frogs toads and crickets, a wall of sound Spector couldn't match. Immature night heron in the last light of the garden, calligraphy in stained glass.

This guy on my finger looks like a comic grasshopper, pale yellow, brown back with wide stripes the color of his belly leading to small black spots at the base of his antennae. Painted on brown eyes, black mandibles and a weird squeak, nervous buzzing flight.

June bugs big bodies and ludicrously small, fast-moving wings barely bear them. They fly into anything, lying there stunned, wondering what they are, hoping it's a dream, no time to fester, lay eggs and die. Where's Gregor?

***

Warm, clear fall sun missed up here in the shade until the frost two weeks ago, followed by the clear sun drying the leaves, and the rain two days ago brought them down. Yesterday the wind finished the job. The ground crackles, the sun shines through, drying the house, first direct light since May.

In the logged-off low gap between Esty's and the Selby farm on the river, two guys are trying to cut their winter wood. I am uphill on the edge of the uncut trees a couple of hundred yards southwest and about a hundred feet above them. One guy is tinkering with his saw, which won't run. He pulls the starter rope. He pulls it again and it whirs, he pulls it whirs, he pulls it whirs, he pulls it a last time and it whirs again. Then it whirs again and I realize how far away I am in the clear autumn air. The dry ground is warm, hairy woodpecker on a hickory seed tree, sassafras bush next to me leaves redolent in the afternoon sun.

Dittany like a tiny shrub, small dry white flowers glowing against blood-brown leaves, and bushy aster blooming all over the low gap. .22 pistol working over an old five-gallon oil can.

Wayne told Bill he was looking for his friend's dogs. Bill said he had heard two dogs up behind his place, one with a fine voice, the other coarse. Wayne reckoned that must be them: an old walker and a young blue tick he'd just bought.

***

The ambulances like to call attention to the fact that they are helping, and that their good intentions give them authority. So the state is good for licensing intention, selling authority on the open market. The ambulance arrived and Randy was long gone to the hospital with John in his truck.

***

The line running down all four tiers to the barn floor is made of tension running down our tired legs and arms holding us in the one place we can stand and hit. So thank you for this rainy day alone in the morning. I can't stand on the slippery barn or dig post holes or Mikki and Lily gone to town, the chickens cooing under the house, me at the desk and so much to come out. Out the window tall, thin, gray rain and hickories combined on the forest green background black cohosh, bellflower, and phlox.

***

Roy says liquors never touched his lips and has the same medicinal bottle he bought in 1910, still sealed. Kinney ran a still and lugged the sugar sacks two at a time over the ridge and clear up Dry Run almost to Polecat Holler. "Been plumb to Washington Court House." He did time for stealing timber from the state and beat the minister with his knucks for insinuating that Kinney was low class because he'd been to prison. Roy and Lucille go to church every week in his Studebaker. Both Kinney's wives left him: two big families. Roy's only son runs the farm. Kinney died and left a hundred acres of deep timber and fallow pasture. A million stories.

***

Snowed in. Snow din: silence. On the roof, more surface than mass, levity lightly falls. Axes, sledges, wedges, and wood, under the weather.

Contrary winter clear cold breakdown. Truck and saw arrested. A longer time between words that haven't been said before. Lily full of snot, hair matted with puke, peristalsis jerked backwards. Clogged throats.

Ice slipping off the roof as the house warms after a week below zero. River frozen for the first time since they put in bigger dams forty years ago. Traffic stopped.

Little white oak (thirty-five feet tall, not quite four inches through at the butt, but "crushed" makes it little) crushed, long fracture up the side. I had to cut up the big beech I had cut down to get it out from under. And winched it straight with the comealong, tied it closed with baling twine. Deep winter keeping her. Post oak, ergo proper oak.

***

Busting beech for Goldie for another jar of sauerkraut. She insists on paying for services rendered, inviting us in for instant Folgers and Cremora, ninety degrees and no oxygen or light, army blankets over the doorways and windows, Buckeye full of the last coal in town. A hundred years worth of photographs: grandparents, mother, Ernie, Melvin, Everett and she behind myriad nieces and nephews. They're kids, and then their kids. Goldie is too, lumps on her breast and thigh she showed Gayle while Ronny and I saw and split in the beautiful air below freezing since Christmas.

Walking from the well, waterbuckets trailing the top of the snow. Scared up two big hawks. They called over and over and flew at me, unwilling to relinquish something I couldn't find in the snow and honeysuckle on the bank.

***

Swinging around a clifty place, stepped on a rotten rock and it broke. Fell five or six feet onto my tailbone, barely made it out of the woods, dizzy with pain and fear that I'd hurt myself permanently.

Trying to work and favor a sore tail: carrying unsplit osage orange posts up hill at Roger's, lifting a Chevy 235 head and all into the back of a flatbed with Ronny and Randy, floating a footer and carrying block, all with the same grimace, squatting to shit. Laughing too hard at Cruiser's blues grass jazz breaks, rolled over backwards and roared with pain and joy.

***

Stringing wire with Roy and Roger along the south bank of the slough below the alfalfa field. First daisy fleabane, redwing blackbirds in the hackberry, one gliding across the slough slow motion in front of me. Thick rotten splinter just solid enough to jam under the callous of my thumb. Roger and Roy both relaxed and friendly with me, but tired of each other after forty-eight years of being father and son.

I told Roger I thought he was too concerned with good looks in women, rather than the good looks they might give him, and he told me that he wasn't what he seemed. He was right, but what does he seem? They flee from me who sometimes make me sick.

Reusing old barbed wire, cobbling or coddling the fence, slipping in rotting driftwood and feminine hygiene spray bottles, the wire snapped around and caught Roy's finger deep, stuck there in its will to recoil. I cut the wire away as Roy issued conflicting instructions about the best way to free him, blood pumping down his hand, but as soon as he was free he went right back to work. Eighty-five years of it. At 5:30 Roger called it off because Roy was tired, slippery sidehill footing, but Roy was the only one who didn't want to quit.

Stopped by Essman's on the way home to borrow the big tiller, watched Lawrence and Lewis, father and son milking the cows like two bodies with one mind, came home to beets, eggplant, and rice, and plowed the garden until I couldn't see where I was going.

Goldie called Joyce for a man; so I went up to help hold Ginger while Old Doc

Carr looked her over. I got there just after dark and Goldie was waiting on the porch with two flashlights. We found Ginger standing miserable behind the old schoolhouse, favoring her left hindquarter. We got the bridle on her, a tangle of leather in the dark, and compared notes until Randy got there with Lloyd and Johnny in tow. She jerked every place he touched her, though she let me hold the bridle, fondling her neck and crooning to her. When Doc Carr came he said it was hornets, great welts on her sides, swollen in every joint. Old Doc had been treating Ginger for twenty-six years and she was shy but let him slide his hand along her neck, needle between his index and middle fingers, syringe hanging loosely over the back of his hand. When he found the vein he continued massaging her neck with his right hand while his left slowly pushed in the plunger. She never trembled. Then he said to take her to the creek. Randy led her in until her back went under and she began dipping her head and blowing water. After a few minutes we were afraid she'd get pneumonia and led her back to the pasture. Johnny closed the gap and we left her under the trees, still steaming.

***

I could hear a storm coming through the trees over the hill behind us, raced down the hill unhooked the goat and wet-footed it back up, raining cats and catch canning us just past the sandbox.

Back again in the bower after the rain stops, work begins in a light breeze, a touch of blue in the sky the open window and green distant sound of voices as people first children come out of the houses.

***

She said to her mother, "Let's pretend that you're my mother and I am your daughter." Which startled and delighted her, but it was reasonable that she might pretend to be herself. It is the essence of adventure, and the opposite of rapture, when you know you are somebody else, the lost singular you that mothered me.

***

Spring flowing from under the linden tree. Sharp screeing redtails overhead. First quarter hepatica cranesbill and ginger, stem ends of linden flowers in the spring.
Breaking twigs and shredding dead leaves. Damp cool ground, ass and elbow. Tiny translucent ginseng under cover. Newt in a poplar stump. Head downhill, taking the load off.
Hummingbird stuck in Dawn's back room, banging into the glass until I was

able to cage it in my hands, red in its throat brightened by black above and below. It weighed nothing, then I let it go.

***

Four snakes and a beetle: the first lying halfway across the road across from Everett's, distended with egg after egg or mousies but lumps along its length. I tossed pebbles at its head until it slipped into the weeds so the car could pass. The second I saw the same day coiled in the road up Worley's Run, then gone by the time I could stop. Coming back down I saw old Swords with a stick to finish off the snake his daughter had run over. That's why it was coiled. The next day Brad ran one out of the woodpile and today Keith and Bubby saw one in a rotting windrow. John came out and set the hay on fire and clubbed the snake with a spud bar when it fled. He held it up shoulder high on the bar and it hung double to his knee.

Painting the eaves, bat in the corner, polyphemous on the door, a huge monarch flickered past me under the overhang. Rhino stag on the concrete, waving helpless hopeful legs in the air. Each day I turned him over for pity, then turned him back over because we were both so worthless.

Coda: Jake stomps a snake. I got pissed. I held it in as much as possible, but it still showed. They were bewildered. You have to get along in the tobacco patch. It was a garter snake, coiled in the shade of a tobacco leaf from the noonday sun.

***

The use of binoculars: changing the oil yesterday, the faint but unmistakable sound of geese calling their way north. I scanned the sky as much as the bright haze would permit, but no sign and the sound grew fainter and fainter. I ran in and got the field glasses and started scanning the northern horizon and finally, about twenty degrees above the ridge, the glasses picked up two long lines: a straggly vee and a thin, attenuated following line. There must have been a hundred of them going home on the horn. Then the morning sky through Ben's glasses, the Grand Curve from Saturn to Venus, Mercury implausible in the eastern haze. Winds pulsing through the poplars along the run like waves unfolding on a beach against the low, constant keen of the oaks as the wind cups the ridge.

***

Mockingbird descends in a white-barred flutter, looks over the lawn around the big swamp oak, then up to the electric wire. He throws a few fakes, tail twitching, on balance, and loses himself in the oak leaves. Blackbirds, thrushes, wrens, cardinals, swallows: I hear them all around. Which ones are being mocked?

The spruce by the old homestead on the river towers above the scrub willows that line the bank. From the ridge it spans the river in the upper half of the painting. It's a vista: five-hundred feet vertical and a thousand yards to the water glistening in the 4 P.M. winter solstice sun only ten degrees above the ridge on the south bank.

***

Closing the shop when a car skidded into the driveway and a nimbusheaded guy jumped out: "O God come help me, Buddy. I've shot my friend." I hopped in my truck and followed him back out to the road. Just before we turned up Sunshine, Jeff came through the gap and rolled down his window to talk, "follow us" after the guy who waited at each curve until I came into sight then tore away. A couple of miles out Sunshine Ridge he pulled off on the right, killed the engine and ran into the brush, beckoning as he went. A quarter mile into the woods, just where the ridge drops off into Southdown, he dropped beside a man hunched on the ground, moaning deep and constant, the left thigh of his jeans purple and a dark, dirty hole slowly pumping venous blood sopped into his pant leg.

"Help me get my belt off, my leg just flops." His thighbone was shattered too high in the crotch to tourniquet. We cinched his legs together and Jeff took his feet as the other guy and I locked hands under his back, no time to devise a stretcher, we lugged him through rock briar patches saplings and honeysuckle until he stopped us because the pain was too great, but only for a minute until the blood oozing off his jeans made us pick him up again. Twice we did that out to the road and my truck, and we slid him in the back on some cardboard. I drove as carefully as I could back out the ridge and down to Jody's, who grabbed blankets and towels and rode in back with the guy all the way to the hospital in West Union, stanching the wound with a towel and trying to keep him warm. I called the hospital that night, but he had been taken to Cincinnati and there was no further information.

***

Saturday morning, Bud woke us up with his repeated barking. I went to Zoe's window and saw him at first light, staring up hill. When I got up an hour later, he was gone. I called for him and all day alerted the neighbors that my beagle dog was lost and dragging his chain.

I got up early the next day and started up the hill. At the first bench, I pondered and decided that he'd been looking more toward the south and the river than toward Tucker's Run on my north; so I started around the face of the hill up the draw behind Duke's to the long flat bench and from the top of the south face the Ohio six hundred feet below me snaking between the ridges toward Vanceburg broad, steel blue in the early light. Then away from the river through the saddle to the next peak in the ridge, calling down into the bowls of hickory and oak that led steeply away into rills running down into Dry Run on my left hand or Tucker on my right. I became aware, gradually then all at once that I could barely hear a dog barking away off down toward Dry Run. Pete seemed to want to head that way, understandably, and I started down through the greenbriers, thinking it was probably the yard shitters tied up behind Tom Lewis's out on 52, just before it enters Upper Twin about a mile from the end of Twin Creek's meander across the flood plain to the Ohio.

I kept dropping down the draw thinking that and that whatever ground I gave up heading down hill would have to be regained later, and at the same time the pattern of the faint barks seemed familiar and a small hope that Bud wouldn't starve to death wrapped on his chain around a briar or a grapevine or china root or, most likely, all three and a sassafras sprout.

It became clear that I was heading down the holler where Kinney said he'd kept his still under an eight-foot-deep ledge, the first time I'd approached it from the ridge. By then the barking had stopped and I was worried that whatever dog it was had travelled around the face of the hill away from me, which meant it couldn't have been Bud. Then I realized that Pete was gone, and that I had little choice but to drop with the rill down through the rock ledges, huge beech separating the water course into two strands, so steep I held saplings to keep from sliding on my ass in the leaves, careful of twisting an ankle in the rocks. As I came down past Kinney's cave, the hillside broadened into the bench where years ago I had found the rock with a glyph of a claw in cameo relief on one face, and I could hear Bud barking excitedly.

I found him wrapped in just the assortment of vines and sprouts that I had imagined. He had trailed something under a grapevine, then back over it, around a hickory sapling, and back under the grapevine. His homemade bowline was cinched into his chain so tight that I had to unleash him to get it free. He immediately began to cast wide after the scent he'd been on twenty-four hours earlier when he'd got bound up. He didn't even stop to take a piss. I kept calling him and, as soon as he was convinced that the trail was cold, he came straight back and jumped in my lap. I snapped him back up and snubbed the chain around my waist. He pulled me all the way back around the face of the hill past the tree farm, Kersey's, Humble's, and Duke's, back across the run I was choking him back from dragging me through the brambles until finally I could see the cabin way below me through the woods. On down, snapped him back on his run, and finally into the house to get his breakfast, and my own.

Ohio River at Cincinnati riverfront ©Charles Cassady Jr.

KEVIN WALZER

KEVIN WALZER was born in Cooperstown, New York in 1968. He lived in New York, Georgia and Kentucky before moving to Cincinnati, Ohio in 1981. Walzer graduated from Ohio University in 1990 with bachelors' degrees in English and journalism, and is currently studying for a Ph.D. in English at the University of Cincinnati. In addition to being a poet, critic and essayist, he is associate editor of *Cincinnati Poetry Review*. He is currently completing a collection of poems entitled "Made Light."

"Cincinnati: A Note from the Province" is not so much an autobiographical essay about a young man's coming of age as it is his coming of vision; or, better yet, expanded vision. Here, Walzer's focus is Cincinnati, a city he scorned from his comfortable suburban lifestyle until he went away to college and later married a woman from the "other side" of the city. It is an essay about a provincial person—"someone so saturated with a world that they can't imagine anything outside it"—who emerges from a part of the city to see, understand and accept the whole of the city.

CINCINNATI: A NOTE FROM THE PROVINCE

June 1981. Twelve years old, I climbed into my father's wheezing brown Honda. My friend Mark, with whom I'd been staying, stood on his front porch and waved. I waved back as we pulled away. My brothers—Eric, 10, and Dan, 4—were in the back seat. I sat in front with my dad, Peter. We'd join my mom, Kathleen, at the end of the trip.

Soon we were on Interstate 75, leaving behind Lexington, Kentucky, for Cincinnati. It was the fourth state I would live in.

I was happy to leave Lexington. I was born in New York, which had make me feel superior to anyone from Kentucky. I wore my condescension like a sweatshirt. But the Kentucky rednecks bit back. I was the brainy seventh-grade geek whom all the loose girls make fun of, a "pudgy, four-eyed, booger-eating" 12-year-old. A thin-skinned, dreamy type who wanted to be a bestselling author, I wrote self-pitying poems that proclaimed my agony to the world. I cried almost every day that year, over one insult or another. I made straight A's and was miserable.

As I sat simmering with these thoughts, the interstate began to slope and turn like a roller coaster. I looked out the window. High walls of layered stone guided the road, which had been gouged out of the earth like a crater. We were nearing the Ohio River. Bridges linked Kentucky to the backdrop Cincinnati skyline: Riverfront Stadium, Carew Tower, the Central Trust building.

I couldn't wait to cross the river.

My parents had bought a house in Kenwood, an upper-middle-class suburb near ritzy shopping malls. On moving in, I thought, *Hmm. This is more civilized.* But that didn't prepare me for where I would attend school that August, at the dawn of Ronald Reagan's "Morning in America." The Village of Indian Hill, Exempted, was a semi-rural, hilly, forested town a few miles from Kenwood where the wealth was so great it was nearly invisible; behind hedges facing the narrow, twisting roads stood mansions overlooking three-, five-, and ten-acre properties, with long driveways, three- and five-car garages, tennis courts, swimming pools. Indian Hill, I would later discover, had one of the highest per capita incomes in Ohio, and was home to Cincinnati's elite: senior Proctor and Gamble executives, financiers, lawyers, business owners, athletes. They favored the imperial understatement of old money, rather than the gaudy display of the nouveau riche more common in Kenwood.

Their children, with whom I attended school, were well-spoken, refined, outfitted in fashionable clothes, competitive, and mostly conservative. They had endless allowances to spend as they chose. When they turned sixteen, most would get cars, some BMWs or Corvettes. When they turned 18, they would all attend college, mostly private: Harvard, Yale, Northwestern, Oberlin. When I first met them, I was dazzled, and humbled. Here was the real elite. Though my house, too, had a pool, I felt poor. And, having just come from Kentucky, backward.

Like most children, I was shaped by my immediate surroundings—my affluent neighborhood, and my absolutely rich high school. I wanted desperately to fit in with that school's bright, smooth, successful teenagers. Thanks to my grandmother, Eileen Walzer, a journalist and fiction writer, I already had an interest in writing. Partly to stoke this interest, and partly to fit in, I plunged into school publications. First I contributed to the middle school newspaper. Then, in ninth grade, I joined the high school paper and gradually absorbed the overriding Indian Hill ethic: That paper was *mine*! My byline appeared everywhere. In the grinding, cutthroat environment of Indian Hill, journalism was a place where I was literally *better than anyone else*—a fact that counted even more than income, or potential income.

By that point, I was completely of Indian Hill: saturated with elitism, ambition, and wealth. Publicly, I meekly echoed my parents' liberal views—I was the lone Walter Mondale supporter in my American history class—but I secretly envied the riches that seemed to attend the conservative Republican values dominating the country: the huge five-acre houses, the BMWs, the Gucci shoes, and Ralph Lauren suits my friends' fathers wore. In *The New York Times Magazine*, I read of young supply-siders, fresh from economic majors at Princeton or Harvard, making $80,000 in their first years on Wall Street. I watched *Lifestyles of the Rich and Famous*, and for a while patterned my own lifestyle after the richest and most famous man on TV, Don Johnson of *Miami Vice*; I started wearing pastel red and blue T-shirts under unconstructed, white *faux*-linen sports jackets, topped off with cheap mirror sunglasses and unkempt stubble.

At 17, with few of the insecurities I had brought over the Ohio River from Kentucky, I though the world was mine. After touring 11 colleges, including Yale,

Brown, and Oberlin, I divided to attend Ohio University, a public university. I boasted to all my Indian Hill friends that I'd be entering OU's selective honors tutorial program. I would be majoring in English and journalism at a program rated in the top ten nationwide by the Associated Press. That, I told everyone, would enable me to get a job at a major daily newspaper—probably *The Boston Globe* or *The Miami Herald*, if not *The New York Times*. I predicted that in 10 years I'd have two Pulitzers and be an elite, successful professional, just like my friends bound for pre-law at Duke or pre-med at Dartmouth. I would always carry the standards of Indian Hill High School with me, I thought—and I would make the people there proud.

What a provincial I was.

When I arrived at Ohio University in September of 1986, I told all the other new students I met that I was from Cincinnati. But that wasn't true. I was from a small, wealthy corner of Cincinnati—Kenwood-Indian Hill. I did not know Cincinnati. When my dad, a medical professor at the University of Cincinnati, asked me to apply there—because it was tuition-free for professor's dependents—I snorted and made no effort to hide my scorn. I thought the University of Cincinnati was the dumping ground for mediocre Indian Hill students—those who couldn't get in anywhere else. I grudgingly applied, then visited the school—and was horrified. It was so *urban*. All that concrete. No trees. All those tough-looking, urban hoods walking the streets in the surrounding neighborhood. Ugh. No way would I go there.

Though I didn't know it then, *that* was Cincinnati. Or at least a big representative slice of it—the complex rhythm of life in a big Midwestern city. People everywhere. Buildings thrown up for function, not tranquility. No time or space for walks on a three-acre lawn.

I wasn't from *there*.

Actually, at the time, I didn't know really where I was from. I didn't think about it. I didn't think of how my world, tiny as it was, had shaped me.

But it's impossible, or at least real hard, to do that from *inside* a world. That is what defines the provincial person: someone so saturated with a nearby world that they can't imagine anything outside of it. Though I was affluent and ambitious, I was no less provincial than any other stereotypical Ohioan: a farmer from Wilmington, a steelworker from Youngstown, a coal miner from Ironton, a kid from Kenwood.

That changed.

Moving to another province—Athens, a small liberal town in the Appalachian foothills of Southeastern Ohio—helped. The experience of friends struggling to afford the modest (to me) tuition at OU showed me how lucky I was. Some just didn't have as much money as I. Some, either out of pride or family difficulty, were financially independent. Others, from the Appalachian towns outside Athens, struggled to escape real poverty that existed in their families for generations. The experiences of my friends, so different from mine, showed me that my lot was only a small, privileged one in a large world.

Another factor that helped: dating, then marrying, my wife, Lori Jareo. Lori, who attended OU with me, was also from Cincinnati. Whenever the academic term ended, we drove back together to Cincinnati over Ohio 32, the James A. Rhodes Appalachian Highway, a long, curving, hilly four-lane freeway running through Ohio's rural South. I began to think of Cincinnati as a place we shared, *our* city. Driving to her house—all the way on the city's far west side, the other side of town from Kenwood—showed me a good deal of that place.

In Cincinnati, there is a clear division between the east and west sides of the city. The East—typified by Indian Hill—is the affluent, educated elite. The West Side is Cincinnati's bedrock, comprised largely of white, middle- and working-class families—often the foot soldiers of Cincinnati's dominant Republican party, as opposed to its East Side financiers. From the East Side point of view, West Siders are uncouth, industrious but unpleasant. Two of Indian Hill's most prominent residents, baseball hit king Pete Rose and Cincinnati Red's owner Marge Schott—both born and raised on the West Side, but wanting the good Indian Hill life their fortunes enabled—stuck out like sore thumbs.

Driving Interstate 275, the loop around Cincinnati, I shed my stereotypes about the West Side. It was nearly an hour drive from Kenwood to Lori's Monfort Heights neighborhood. The landscape of half my city, which I had never seen before, actually differed little from the East Side: tacky strips of stores and fast-food joints; cul-de-sacs of manicured lawns and neatly painted houses. Driving the same route so many times, I gained a sense of knowing *all* of Cincinnati. And because I also began to identify Cincinnati with Lori and me, not just myself, the city became especially important to me.

It is a bit embarrassing to admit that Cincinnati is important to me now, since Lori and I currently live here. It is embarrassing because there are many people—nationwide, but also in Ohio—who regard our city as a monolith of hidebound provinciality, of which my own is a tiny but typical example.

I know. The nation sees Cincinnati as a capitol of close-mindedness. We prosecute art galleries for obscenity. We allow the Ku Klux Klan to erect Christmas crosses on our city's landmark, Fountain Square (though not without protest). We blindly worship baseball's all-time hits leader, Rose, because he so embodies Cincinnati values—hard work, perseverance—even though his off-field gambling disgraces the game (and city). We excuse the racial and religious slurs of Reds' owner Schott—who singlehandedly built a fortune in car dealerships after her husband's death—for the same hometown reasons. We also forgive robber baron Charles Keating, who chased smut out of Cincinnati in the 1950's.

All these vices cannot be denied. They are part of the recent historical record. Even though they embarrass me, and many Cincinnatians, others see no problem with them—which is part of the problem, a people ingesting its stereotype.

But vices are often pursued to excess. In returning to Cincinnati after college, in choosing to make it my home, I have come to understand this point: Cincinnati's vices are part and parcel of its virtues.

Cincinnatians *do* tend to worship hard work, perseverance, and loyalty to family. These values, historically (though not essentially) associated with Republicans, are the reason Hamilton County is such a bastion of Republican politics. These values permeate life in this city; they are part of its cultural fiber, impossible to dislodge. I suspect they emerged from the German immigrants who settled the city in the early 1800s, and who still form the West Side culture that East-siders scorn—but which also still largely defines the character of the city.

These values do not encourage cosmopolitanism. All too often, they lead to provinciality—a narrow-mindedness far worse than the kind I displayed as a teenager, the kind that led to the persecution of Dennis Barrie as the art director of the Contemporary Arts Center for featuring the photography of Robert Mapplethorpe, some of which depicted violent homoerotic acts: bullwhips and fists rammed up anal passages. A violent affront to traditional morality. They *were* shocking and offensive. And also brilliant art which the city prosecutor had no business trying to censor.

But the traditional ideology of work, perseverance, and family is not evil. Those who oppose the efforts of homosexual couples to legally marry and raise children do not recognize that homosexuals are trying to make space for themselves *within* the ideology of family. The most zealous Cincinnatians fail to recognize that traditions evolve through time, but those traditions do not, through evolution, lose their force as traditions.

And Cincinnati, at its best, speaks to the value of the traditional ideology of work and family. Whatever his personal flaws—including, I've read, being a less-than-exemplary husband and father—Pete Rose on the baseball field was a glorious embodiment of the work ethic. He was a man of limited athletic gifts. He was hardly the greatest "pure" hitter to play baseball. His breaking Ty Cobb's record for career hits resulted as much from endurance as talent; his career batting average was significantly lower than Cobb's, but his endurance—his perseverance, his drive—was the point. Sprinting to first base on walks, sliding headfirst and hard, he never backed down. He wrung every ounce of his ability on the field, and the rest was effort. "Charlie Hustle," indeed. Who could fail to be inspired by such sights, even with knowledge of the conduct that banished him from the game? And can one blame some Cincinnatians for letting the pride he brings the city blind them to his disgrace?

I am *of* Cincinnati now. I am now working on a Ph.D. in English at the University of Cincinnati—the school I scorned years ago. I have shed my Kenwood-Indian Hill provinciality and joined a larger community: the whole of Cincinnati.

Cincinnati's values have value. This is my province.

Couple gazing at downtown Cincinnati
from heights of Eden Park ©Charles Cassady Jr.

CONSTANCE PIERCE

CONSTANCE PIERCE teaches creative writing at Miami University in Oxford, Ohio. Her works include *When Things Get Back to Normal*, a collection of stories, and *Philippe at His Bath*, a collection of poetry, as well as essays on photography, film, landscape ecology, and various literary subjects. She has received two National Endowment for the Arts Fellowships for fiction and a Logan Award for New Writing on Photography. She has recently co-edited a book, *Elvis Rising*, an anthology of contemporary fiction that features "The King."

What happens to the person who loves the proximity of the ocean, but must move "inland" to the prairies and flatlands of Ohio and Indiana to live? In the case of Constance Pierce, she is "transformed" by the experience. A writer looking for a place to "connect to," she finds it, to her surprise, on the border between Indiana and Ohio—a place between two places, but still it is "some place," she writes, "particular and distinctive."

ON BEING LANDLOCKED

When I came to teach in southwestern Ohio in 1980, I followed a route familiar to the pioneers, from Pennsylvania, where I had lived in the middle of the state, in a climate that produced each season at its expected time, in its expected guise. There, all flowers bloomed, as expected, in spring, little variance year to year. My pretty Pennsylvania town was small but large enough, and isolated enough, to provide most of the goods and services and entertainments that a person would want. It was buffered from the worst effects of weather by low-lying hills and (indeed) a sylvan geography. It was protected from marauders (if not always from itself) by a lack of proximity to an Interstate or airport or major city. It was a place that could seem ideal, as homogeneous university towns often do. Even those who felt marooned there—unfairly rusticated by a tight academic job market and quarantined from their natural peers in the higher ivory towers—tried not to be bitter. Even in their feelings of entrapment and isolation, they knew that this was a landscape with undeniable physical virtues, and so they routinely spoke about this place where they had ended up with an amused irony, and called it by an arcadian name: "Happy Valley."

What they silently faulted was that this was not the home of one of the great universities of the East, that it was not New York City, a "cultural center."

Of course, cable television eventually brought New York City itself right into our homes, red in tooth and claw. The lurid Metromedia ten o'clock news was a nightly trauma. The world—finally, as predicted—seemed to have begun its briefing for a descent into Hell, starting with New York, which was only 200 miles away.

New York...my old and my (now, that I was moving to Ohio, it looked like for good) never-to-be-achieved Oz.

This was how I was thinking as I packed up for my new job in Ohio—a little wistful, moving west. I exacerbated the fearsome effects of the ten o'clock news, in the hope of a miracle of resignation. Maybe terror, and the promise of its relief, would stave off the more difficult emotion, always threatening: dread.

Why dread?

Well, first and most important, Ohio was very far inland. Born in Virginia and raised in North Carolina, I had never lived more than a few hours' drive from the Atlantic Ocean. Several times I had lived on its shores, and had once actually lived surrounded by it. (This came with its own difficulties, but that is another story.) Even my temporary home in Pennsylvania was fairly close to that body of water. Blue crabs were trucked in from Baltimore every week to crawl around the walls of our seafood store; nearby, live clams and oysters hunkered down in chipped ice.

Of course dread was not about the loss of ready seafood, though this was important. No, the more important thing was that, even in the middle of Happy Valley, a person could get in a car and, in three hours, be at the Atlantic Ocean— my crucial orientation since I'd first visited its shoals and beaches at a very young age. As a young adult, not even "New York City" could have compelled me, I don't think, without its physical location on that ocean.

This orientation to seemingly limitless water and horizon (how *primary* it can seem, even when it's secondary, not-native) is not always easy to explain to people who live inland and are differently moored, and happily so. For someone oriented to, longing for, an ocean, there is a deep unease that comes with the notion of being "landlocked." It deepens incrementally as a farther inland yet is imagined. This is not particularly logical, is in fact almost inexplicable. It's not a matter of safety, because a shoreline is a dangerous place. It is not a matter of comfort, for the very ground near an ocean, at least in summer, is inhospitable, fiery underfoot—a medium in which little of use will grow. The connection a person makes to an ocean and its shores occurs deep within, where regular rhythms beat and waves other than those of the brain obtain. The sense, and the feeling, is located in a mid-region, in a sort of...Heartland.

The best I can do is describe how the ocean affected me on first sight: It was where water met horizon in the far, unfathomable distance. In effect, the site of *release*. Which is to say, I suppose, that it was the only place that I knew where limitations became invisible.

The prairies and flatlands of the Midwest must have similar effects on others.

Of course, the shift in physical geography was not the whole source of impending dread, as I prepared to relocate. No, as ("upstairs") I contemplated Ohio, I could half-tell that I was also trying to forestall my own sense of being rusticated, as my Pennsylvania colleagues felt themselves to be, "landlocked" in a figurative way. Like them, I was caught up in prejudices that are hard to avoid, if you're a literary type. In much of the literary history that I knew, the migration of writers had been *away* from the Midwest, and the writers, once flown, had told devastating tales out of school. What I knew first-hand, at that time, of Ohio and the Midwest, I'd gathered passing through in a car in the dead of night. What I knew in the power of imaginative detail I had from the disaffected, Dreiser to Lewis to Scott Fitzgerald to Gass.

But as I packed up, I was also being bombarded with a particular mode of TV commercial that was prevalent then, for lemonade and such, even for a cereal called Heartland. These featured the happy generations mingling in summertime, clearly in the Midwest: The sweating pitcher on the gingerbready porch, the flag flapping on its pole...

I didn't, couldn't, trust that! But—

Ohio...it *would* be green with corn, isolated from the terrors of Metromedia, and safe. Happy Valley...without the valley. Without the Slough of Despond.

The primary feature of the Midwest, and Ohio, is arguably its flatness. (Also true of the southatlantic coastal plains, but this was harder to see back then.) Though a beautiful feature to the farmer who must work intimately with the ground, for the rest of us, such flatness challenges our esthetics and our imaginations. And with flatness comes not isolation, but exposure. At least, at the physical level. This I would learn soon enough.

Out here, the winds were often high and relentless, I discovered; the uprooting of trees was a common thing, the devastation of houses not far behind. Some flowers bloomed in some springs, some in others, some once and never again. The thunderheads and lightning miles away were brought closer to the eye as it looked out on an uninterrupted terrain, often flat as a spatula. The long flat roads that cut across Ohio exposed one to a dangerous regional style of driving, constant tailgating, every driver emboldened by his clear view ahead. The sky at night was dark, and vast, unbroken by anything darker than itself—no hills; in the more agricultural regions, not much in the way of trees—exposing the emotions to cosmic indicators better left unexpressed. As for earthly terrors, so flat was the ground that you didn't even need an antenna, much less a cable, to bring Cincinnati and Dayton and Indianapolis into your house, giving Metromedia a run for its money.

"Out Here." It is a phrase common to the newly transported. It betrays a foot still deeply planted in the East. ("Out" in North America is always west, isn't it?) It presumes a "cultural center" (always on the edge of the continent, not "central" at all) from which one has been exiled. "Out Here"—exiled from the meaningful fringe...to The Heart of It All: the Heart of the Heart of the Country, the Heart of Darkness.

"Out Here" speaks to a sense of physical and notional isolation that can seem bred in the bone, though it is the result of a long history of insinuations, presumptions, landscape esthetics that view flatness as estranging and see the happier emotions in rise and gorge (and possibility in large bodies of water?).

Further, for those newly from elsewhere, Ohio is a place where they don't yet know anybody, and much prior information is foreboding: Babbitts, boosters,

Republicans...

Kent State didn't happen in our state.

American Gothic is nothing we care to encounter.

Many arrive only to declare that "in a couple of years" they'll be moving elsewhere.

Speaking for myself—arriving in summer, seeing that the corn was green, making a first pitstop in Zanesville, where gingerbread porches were in abundance, flags battered poles, and a paddlewheel boat plied the River Muskingum draped in red, white and blue bunting—though these should have discomfited, given my generation's skepticism—I felt frantically elated. Further west, at my destination, I moved into a 19th-century farmhouse with its own gingerbread (which, it should now be confessed, was a couple of miles across the State Line Road, into darkest Indiana—a state further inland yet). This house evoked Grant Wood's famous Gothic house, a little, but rather charmingly. Each morning I rose to watch the mists rise above a little creek (actually, a drainage ditch full of chemical run-off from the fields, but I didn't know that yet). The rising sun lit up the tips of the barncats' hair. Everything was rising! Not the least my spirits, my conviction that this had been a good move. My part of this part of the country, approaching the Ohio River, wasn't even entirely flat. The corn was a veritable sea, stretching out to Wyoming—at least. Having not yet seen the Imperial Valley of California, this valley-less Midwest displayed agriculture conducted on a scale I'd never before witnessed. And yet, comfortingly, the family farm—not yet entirely into the crisis that was imminent—was its mainstay.

Every evening I boiled no less than thirteen ears of sweet corn, contented with the citizens of the region by so small, or large, a thing as the corn-seller's bonus ear against worms. Never mind that the electricity went out for hours the first night in my new home. A neighbor drove over in his pickup, unbidden, and brought a flashlight. A good sign. An elemental neighborliness that life in Happy Valley had eluded.

Naturally, these euphorias couldn't go on, but the Midwest—in that season, and in the seasons to come when agriculture pursued its necessary rhythms and endured the discord of inclement weather and brutal economics—achieved for me a lasting interest, a fascination. My mind was eventually restocked with the details of this manifestation of the physical world and of the visible habits of the everyday life here. Incrementally I was transformed, as well as transported. But the abstract world became manifest too. I listened to the radio and a different kind of TV in the off-hours, talk of futures and options—promising words, but new meaning. Eventually, I listened with the farmer's skepticism. If things on TV had seemed unreal before, now they seemed downright insidious in their capacity for distraction from real life. Futures, options—scary words, abstractions with real effects, real limitations, in the world where I now lived. A world where a literal stock market, parallel to the one with the bruising power, went about its increasingly precarious business.

After the corn comes down and the fields are left in stubble or else plowed up in anticipation of the next season, everything in the rural Midwest changes. Field mice head for basements and begin to gnaw at wires and wood, die in the walls and give off their sickening perfume for weeks. A certain grimness lies over things. The Grant Wood houses all around my county seem secretive, containers of truncated lives, as Wood intended to portray. (I see instead: the general truncation of Life, a thing that never seems quite to live up to itself.)

The thin light of March, falling unbroken over the plowed-up fields, makes me—like Huck—so lonesome I could die.

I have never felt such debilitating depression as in these off-seasons, when everything to do with growing things (the work and business of this place) can seem to be shut down.

And yet the farmer's work goes on, the tending of livestock in muddy or icy fields, the maintenance of outbuildings, the recalculation of drainage and loan interest. Everything looks to be in pain—the hogs with their exposed skin, pink and hairless; the cows herding together in the stormy pasture, exposed—or else, when hay runs low, driven onto a truck bound for the slaughterhouse. Metal roofs, in the winds of these dangerous seasons, make a terrible racket, and sometimes fly off altogether and land in a field, leaving animals or people unsheltered. Shelter itself, under such fierce attack, is difficult to maintain. Mortar crumbles and paint peels with amazing rapidity. Whole inhabited houses, not to mention empty barns, list to the West, or East, as if indistinctly summoned—the effect of excessive groundwater or the unpredicted shifting of the frostline by an increment. The flat fields lose earth that will need to be replenished with chemicals later on. The wind sweeps across the snow, and drifts accumulate car-high on the roads. Waterpipes freeze. Rain seeps down chimneys, busting mortar out of its grooves. Groundhogs burrow up under foundation stones, and cluster-flies come out of their homes in the windowsills into warm human rooms and buzz, buzz, buzz.

Where—I ask myself—could that family of baby snakes that I found hissing and writhing under my mulch last summer be now, growing stronger and more toothsome, except in my basement?

At the social level, lone cars move along the edge of the empty cornfield when I wake up in the wee hours, ever my habit. Who is out there, creeping along? On the way to town one day, I see a groundhog dangling in a noose from a tree-limb. Just as bad, I've discovered the region's own brand of scapegoating. "What's a Buckeye?" an Indiana neighbor asks, telling a joke. When I say I don't know, he says, "A Kentuckian on his way to Detroit who ran out of money." "What's a Hoosier?" someone I know in Ohio asks. When I shrug, knowing that by now I am one, he says, "A Kentuckian on his way to Detroit who ran out of money."

Out Here, I have learned the pejorative of "Hoosier," the intolerance located in place. (But then, in my neck of the woods, near Cincinnati, we all get absorbed into a place invented by merchants, anyway: "The Tristate." A depressing brand of equalization.) Out Here, I—a native of the Blue Ridge Mountains, which might explain or mystify further my early affinity for the Atlantic Ocean—have learned, for the first time, the meaner meaning of "briar," derogatory for Appalachians.

Out Here, I have had some interesting thoughts about the role of my—adored, nostalgized—Appalachia in the imaginations of other Americans. This has been useful for my writing, if nothing else. (Oh, but it has been useful for much else, much else...)

I look at the flat winter ground stretching out to the colorless horizon, on and on. But it is nothing like an ocean. Limits are everywhere implied.

Then, like miraculous morning coming back to the speaker in Dylan Thomas's "Fern Hill," the winds die down and the gentler side of spring comes back to where I live and write:

For a few weeks before the thunderstorms rage or the drought burns up everything green in sight (it's always a toss-up which extreme condition will prevail), there is a tiny respite, and it is enough.

The light grows more substantial. Flowers bloom, though never all of them in any given spring. Unlike Thomas's speaker, I notice the difference. But so what?

Spring restores, as spring is meant to, here as elsewhere. And I am restored and readied to go on again—not by what is indigenous to the region but by what is so rare as almost to be anomalous.

"I'm not from a place," says Manley Pointer, Flannery O'Connor's god-forsaken agent of existentialism, more a Displaced Person than her character in the story with that name. "I'm just from some place near a place."

That's my case, for better or worse. (It might well be yours too.) I live on the Oxford Pike, if you're leaving Brookville, Indiana—but on the Brookville Road, if you're leaving Oxford, Ohio. Where I live and write is at the edge of Ohio, which is also at the edge of Indiana, in some ways part of neither, and "isolated" enough almost not to be part of "The Tristate" (though, of course, I am saved, given residence after all, by living—barely—within a bonafide "viewing area.")

I am both isolated and exposed. But then we live in a world where these two states of being are mixed. To be isolated in a place is to be exposed to the human capacity to terrorize, to take our money and our lives. To expose ourselves can terrorize those around us, who might in turn isolate us or terrorize us or both, wherever we live, as relentlessly as the wind and cold.

The much-discussed longing for community on the part of modern people is the flipside of another longing, perhaps always the more powerful one: to break away and be free, far from community's censure. By now, most of us are from several places, not one, which is a kind of "no place." Of course we are lonely and estranged, being tailgated down the Interstate of life, vertiginous with all the places we've exhausted—and with our dreams of the perfect place, the place where we'll fit, because everyone will be so congenial...so much like us?

In our time, the injunction to the writer to be connected to "place" can assume an annoyingly moralistic tone. It is unrealistic, punishing. It silently proposes that to be from many places weakens writing, or makes for a bogus writer. Or human being. After all, one of the worst things an American can be in real life is a drifter. (But in the movies, one of the most romantic.) Surely, O'Connor wishes to suggest the crime of drifting, its suspect nature, in making Manley Pointer "From some place near a place," his direct name notwithstanding.

But like anybody, I have "roots," however much I've moved around. So do you, oh denizen of a hundred places, postmodern North American though you must remain. We're all born some place and some place forms our early imagery, the roots from which we proceed and which we carry with us, tumbleweeds though we may be. Somewhere along the way, most of us internalize a meaningful, orienting geography, or several, and also an idealized "central" place (cultural or otherwise), or several. We "end up" somewhere, at least to finish out our work lives—if we have luck enough to be continuously employed people. Then there remains only the post-work world, which is nebulous in a culture that reifies work (and—of course—leisure) as ours does. To settle any place is so disorienting an idea for some, in this last phase of life, that a commonly desired "place" is on the road in a Winnebago.

Finally, there is only the place of repose to be chosen, or left to someone else to choose.

This is a major contemporary trajectory. To demand that a living North American in the late 20th century be grounded in a specific place seems odd, pastoral. To imply that a writer should be so is a relatively new phenomenon. Only a few decades ago, we expected expatriation. No doubt it is the nomadic life thrust upon us and the diminishing of each place's distinctiveness in mass life, and our discomfort with those situations, that gives "a sense of place" its didactic power in our time.

I've thought all of this even as I vaguely longed for—not the old, not the familiar, not the heavenly, but—the right (?) place. Terra infirma, terra incognita...

There was a point—about six years ago, I think—when I stopped saying "Out Here."

It happened in a swoop, it seemed, when—as a resident/worker of Indiana/Ohio—I flew into the Cincinnati airport (which is in Kentucky) and then drove toward where I live, realizing that the place felt "right," more or less. I had had a brief, but continuous, history here. Without a doubt, this was where I lived. Since I had never had family here, the place was mine alone, sort of, as if I had chosen or invented it. That gave it a claim on me, gave me a claim on it—but nothing I'd want to *insist* on the literary world as virtuous. In important ways, I remain placeless, alien—or associated with so many places as to be "from no place."

But I am here. There is much, by now, that I like here.

Deep down (an infelicitous phrase, as one moves into later life), I know I am going to stay here.

And why not? By now I've concluded that we all live in a world that nobody in her right mind could really desire calling "home." "Home" is a place that is supposed to reflect us, and a place we're expected to reflect upon. What we earthlings have to call home is by now (has forever been?) a place of debilitating inequities, random ethics, violence and disaffection from the species. "Out Here"—out in the Outer-Space of human moral life—every thinking, reflective person is suffering. Reforming our place, when we can't quite see what to do, when so much is invisible and so much power is at a distance, defeats us in advance of our effort. This carries its own weight of defeat. Our place, our human world, is unkind in big ways, every day. It is threatening, seemingly incorrigible. Our sensibilities are "global" in ways we're only half aware of, and every "place" is already touched by that. Wherever we go or settle, we'll be touched, and touched again, by the Everyplace that is the promise and the threat of the so-called information age, and its commercial applications and ideational content.

Believing that, I feel okay living on a road between two places, not too close to either one. It is a kind of deferral, a demurring, another gesture against limits—very American.

Actually, being so "remote," this place is still some place, particular and distinctive. I still see its features. It still surprises.

But: I am landlocked.

That doesn't hold the terrors I'd anticipated. Maybe it helps that a major river is nearby, making its way to a sea. But then, the ocean doesn't hold all its former charms, either. We grow up, and things flatten out a little. Even the ocean looks flat, unless it's roiling. Those of us not blindly intent on war—which is to say, on subduing territory, whether real or abstract—make peace. It's not a dire compromise, but maturity's own grace, in a land where terminal adolescence is encouraged in countless ways.

When I think about it now, an ocean stretching out to meet the sky is not an image of freedom from limitations (a dubious goal anyway), but it is about limitations so fundamental that we are blind to them. It is an image of a place we cannot inhabit easily or for long, water and air, and we are neither fish nor fowl.

So: I am a land critter, landlocked, on a flat piece of this earth. But I haven't ended up mangled on the equivalent of the Metromedia news yet, and it would be stupid, given what the world looks like Out There, to pretend I'm not blessed here, where I live more or less peacefully and work more or less well and find something in both the natural and built landscapes to interest me every day that passes. Perhaps what has done the most to acclimate me to this mercurial climate does have something to do with community, or communing that is oddly one-sided, and pragmatically so, I think. It comes from my high level of interest in my neighbors' activities, which never abates. It is not the peccadillo or rumor that interests me, but rather the persistence and imagination with which the people immediately around me wrestle with the landscape and its weather, with marauders from the insect world and the world of finance. By now, I have no interest in the car lights that creep along the road occasionally, no interest in bugaboos. But I am very interested in what's going on out in the fields, in the noonday sun and also when the lights of combines and tractors move across the dark. People are out there working with the facts. By now, I can deduce in a general way what they're up to: getting the corn down before the weather shifts, or getting the seed in the ground before another deluge turns the plow-rows to clod. I know their interest in me is limited—a woman living by herself on the edge of their fields, who does nothing of local significance, works in another state. But that's fine. They have been kind to me, as different as we are. They have proved to be more tolerant than I was in my initial dread of them and their place. And they're a cheerful lot, with all the talent and knowledge that anyone who farms successfully must possess. They are nothing like Grant Wood's grim man with his pitchfork, and I hope that I am less like the woman beside him, with the skeptical eyes of a...provincial.

Living here has opened my eyes, in more ways than I can tally.

Of course I am blessed here. It would be arrogant to deny it.

And so, I don't. Happy Valley.

Serpent Mound, Adams County ©Becky Linhardt

JOE NAPORA

JOE NAPORA is a Dayton native who has lived in New York, San Francisco, Canada, Michigan, and Kentucky where he now teaches. He is also a political activist supporting issues of peace and human rights globally and locally, most specifically for Native Americans and Latin Americans. Most recently he has worked to save the Serpent Mound in Southern Ohio which is threatened by economic developers.

Napora's poetry is remarkable for its imagination and diversity, and for its humble confrontative form. His books of poetry include: *tHere* (1978), *Portable Shelter, Tongue and Groove* (1982), *The Walum Olum* (translations of the Delaware Indian classic, 1983), *Scighte* (1987), *Journal of Elizabeth Jennings Wilson* (1987), and *To Recognize This Dying* (1987). He is also an essayist and reviewer.

In "Survival and Resistance" he poses a contrast between Ohio's Indian burial mounds and its nuclear power and weapons industry near Dayton. As always his work is on a human scale as it forces us to confront our own values.

SURVIVAL AND RESISTANCE

"Disappointment especially is a salt mine."
—Robert Bosnak

April 17, 1990

The Miamisburg Indian Mound sits on top of a bluff overlooking the Great Miami River as it flows ten miles south of Dayton on its way to empty into the Ohio River a little down stream from Cincinnati. As you walk toward the stone steps that lead to the top, you get a feel for just what a massive presence it is here: covering over an acre and a half of land, over 54,000 cubic yards of earth make up its construction. At its base a metal plaque informs the curious that the mound was once larger than its present size, 65 feet high and 877 feet in circumference.

There is no plaque revealing the facts about the other massive construction dominating this space above the town and the river. To get that hidden information it is necessary to do a different type of digging than what the archaeologists have done at this mound. It is necessary to uncover layers of useless facts, misleading data, even purposeful mis-information from U.S. General Accounting Office reports and Chamber of Commerce bulletins. To get to where the facts finally reveal their meaning you have to go to the few public interest books and pamphlets that have reported on the weapons plant.

The Mound Laboratory is a 306 acre complex factory employing 2300 workers that in 1987 had a budget of $190,000,000. Built three years after the bombings of Hiroshima and Nagasaki, the plant, operated by the Monsanto Company, produces warhead detonators for atomic weapons and plutonium heat generators for satellites. What is not a secret is how much of the economy of this town is dominated by the plant. But what still remains deeply hidden is how much this industry of death dominates all of our thinking. When I look out at the plant

I get a better sense of why, and why I am here.

The plant sits across from the mound separated by a road also serving the golf course, the park surrounding the mound, and the neighborhoods beyond. Like the Indian mound, this factory does not exist alone, cannot be understood in isolation. The Mound Laboratory is part of a national network organized for the sole purpose of hiding below ground the deadly atomic wastes from atomic weapons production. The network will feed plutonium-contaminated materials to The Waste Isolation Pilot Plant (WIPP) in New Mexico.

The seemingly innocent descriptive phrase "waste isolation" is itself a waste product, an example of how our language is used by scientists and bureaucrats against us all by contaminating truth with deception. Nothing exists in isolation, especially plutonium. Through accident or design, plutonium is aptly named after the Greek god Pluto, the god of the underworld, the god of death. Each particle of plutonium forever maintains its ability to cause cancer in humans. *In human.* And for ever. Or as close to forever as we can contemplate—250,000 years.

The Iroquois Indian tribal council had an operating principle guaranteeing any future social actions would have a sound ecological basis. Community decisions would be made by thinking of the effects that might occur in the future: decisions were measured against the lives of seven generations of people. Plutonium is lethal for 8000 generations. I am five years older than the atomic weapons plant. This mound across from the plant is ancient by most human measuring, about 2500 years old. The effects of the nuclear plant will remain lethal for one hundred times the life of the mound and mine.

My exploration of the mounds has become an exercise into the meaning of time, space, life, and death.

May 26, 1990

The Indian Mounds are stories and death. My pursuit of the meaning of the mounds stems from an intuition that the mounds link together in the imagination, link together in the land, forming out-lines, lines that connect out of themselves and out of ourselves, forming patterns connecting us by taking us out of our ego-self and into our eco-self. The mounds are repositories of wisdom. The philosopher Gregory Bateson defines wisdom as being able to recognize "the pattern that connects." The mounds offer us opportunities to partake in that pattern, to bring the body *in line* with wisdom. To use the root word for yoga, the mounds are a yoking, coupling us in union to them. They point the way for us to confront land and self, partake in the pattern of tension we can call geo-ego: the mounds and us, grounded human beings.

There is a challenge here if we can but hear it, a challenge if we can bear it, a challenge as frightful as sex. Like sex the mounds reveal love through a pattern, an emotional stream flowing from us, into us, joining us to each other. The mounds point to and away from destruction of the false faces of ordinary consciousness. The mounds are points that form lines marking, adorning, the body of this earth. They are out-lines, and death, and life, and sex. They offer us the opportunity for a meditation on what it means to be human.

Lovers, mystics, and poets know that to partake in real union it is necessary to surrender the defenses we place around our ego-self that tries to convince us that it exists for our protection. It is this conviction that we can be protected by forces outside of ourselves that allows us to lend our hands to building the nuclear weapons plant across from the mound. It is this conviction that creates the false face of heroics, a distortion of true heroics that make a lie of the nuclear defense as well as personal emotional defenses against facing the truth.

The mound offers an alternative to the refuge of the weapons made across the road where the refuge is nothing but mass annihilation. This alternative is what I am searching for. It is not the mounds which are incomplete, though obviously they are not what they were. But they are what they are, now. If they are shells, they are shells still significant. If they stand alone, the culture that built and sustained them having slipped from them, abandoning them to time and to us, at least they still stand. And they still define their surroundings. Certainly they do so more than they did two thousand and more years ago. Now they stand out from their surroundings; the disparity of what they were and what has become of the landscape makes them all the more uniquely themselves.

I have to insist that the mounds never were natural. They are made from earth, but it is essential to understand that they are constructed artifacts, embodiments of culture. They were made by people to define the space they occupy as human space. The mounds are art. But now, they are ever more artfully art than they ever could have been before. Now this mound sitting across from the atomic weapons plant proclaims the unnaturalness of all that that plant attempts to define as natural.

The people of Miamisburg who depend on this weapons assembly plant for their livelihood perhaps see this mound as nothing but dirt. It is doubtful that they see it as I do, as an artifact more marvelous than the assemblage of complexes that employ a couple thousand people in the construction of weapons which the people here must have come to accept as necessary, as inevitable, and, worse than all, the ultimate self-deception—as natural. To me this mound stands for all that opposes the forces attempting to convince us that these weapons of death are natural, that it is natural that humans are inherently competitive, that it is natural that to progress upward is possible only by making a ladder from the bones of our brothers and sisters, that we can only see far by standing on the heaped bodies of the innocents. To me this mound is a challenge that I face even as I question the kind of challenge it makes on me.

I know I cannot look clearly across the way to the weapons plant surrounded with barbed wire until I learn to look closely at the mound before me. How does this mound of dirt provoke me? And why? I see myself as another, myself but also another, standing on the grass midway between the weapons plant and the mound. Some people are humbled while contemplating the heavens under a star-lit sky. I am humbled and provoked standing between these structures. Situating myself in the middle is a way of seeing myself from the outside, as another. It is a self-projection and a meditation. I can only ask of myself as a curiosity of the landscape defined by this mound, "What about the man standing before it?"

I look west over the plant and see an atomic sunset. Many Indian tribes referred to the west as the Land of the Dead. And hundreds of years after those stories were created, they came more true that the storytellers could understand. It was on Indian land in Nevada where the first atomic bombs were exploded: artificial sunsets in bursts, eruptions of atomic spermatic splendor. It is on Navajo land where the atomic radioactive tailings are now piled in great mounds, true Mounds of the Dead that are constantly scattered by the winds.

The West was the destination of the souls as they traveled the Milky Way, the path of the dead. The East was the Sunland. This place where I stand defines this essential difference, not exactly life or death but different ways of living and different ways of dying. The choices are choices having to do with heroics, with making a livelihood, with seeing clearly, living sanely. I turn to the mound.

This mound, no matter how much is known about it, is not fully known. It is mystery and it is sacred. Or it is nothing but dirt. It sands about 65 feet high, covering over an acre and a half, containing over 54,000 cubic yards of earth. The engineer, the mathematician, statistician, whoever found it necessary to express the grandeur of this mound in numbers, that person is now a number, at best a memory. The mound remains. This fact is elemental.

With full felt knowledge of the frailty of human existence contrasted with the endurance of the mound is how this great earthen construct must be approached and coaxed into revealing itself. The numbers are meant to impress us for the numbers express labor. The numbers express what was accomplished by people we consider to be primitive but who had organized their lives to allow them the leisure to leave this monument for us—a monumental fiction, symbolizing death but promising life.

But the impressive numbers are more than what they seem to signify. They overwhelm us; they numb us. We marvel at them but cannot comprehend their meaning. The builders of these mounds were not overwhelmed. They built, dug, lifted, hauled, dumped, formed, shaped their monuments. We can only resist not being overwhelmed by participating in their building, and we cannot do that. We are numbed by our numbers, by our lack of participation, our concrete participation, in our own monuments. What monuments are they?

They are more than the legacy of atomic wastes, more than toxins, more than mere matter. They are negative monuments, signifying a wastage of spiritual, emotional, agricultural, and economic capital that we have squandered. They are the debts that our lives sink into. Who can comprehend that a Michael Milken makes $500 million a year? Who can really understand that a film called *Pretty Woman* which glorifies a lifestyle of someone we cannot comprehend grosses $59 million in its first week? The news readers and news makers go numb.

I ask myself how I can justify my interest in these mounds during the economic crisis that the Savings and Loan robberies have precipitated. I don't know. The mounds promise through the absence of obvious meaning an uncovering of a communal act not intimate to destruction. But I have no idea what that act might be. I have only the negative guidelines of my own culture to point the way.

March 11, 1989

Nine days before spring, the day is sunny, warm, 19 C / 66 F. The weather cooperates with my imagining the group celebration that must have been happening at this place at the time, the space filled with people from the river to the hill, two thousand or so years ago as this mound was being built. There isn't much visible activity in this town now. And nothing I imagine about this town equals the scenes that I easily create, or perhaps recall, from the distant past.

Miamisburg is a clean little town with well-kept homes. Middle class and prosperous in appearance, it is a nearly picture-perfect mid-western town. But the appearance is deceptive. What appearance is not? To answer that question is why I have come to these mounds. The town's prosperity is built upon the biggest industry, the Mound Atomic Energy Processing Plant. The plant reveals nothing of its function, of course. There are *No Trespassing* signs and small black and yellow atomic energy warning signs. But it is the sign signifying nothing that is the sign of these times.

The community dismisses, ignores, or defends the function of the plant just as it ignores this mound sitting on the hill overlooking the town and the plant. I am sure that the city fathers would explain away any criticism of the plant just as they would try to haul away the mound for fill if there was an immediate profit to be made by doing so. But the mound resists exploitation; the mound just sits atop the hill in a deep silence with a profound simplicity offering little to the imagination of a developer. This mound has escaped even the ravages of the Savings & Loan land speculators and the politicians who aided them.

The mound sits as an advertisement to death, but it is a death the realtors, developers, bankers, and borrowers cannot accept because it has provided the town with jobs. The plant appears full of life. The mound appears dead; it is, so the archaeologists tell us, a monument to the dead. Here is the contradiction we must work ourselves through to see the mounds for what they might mean, for what we might mean. The plant appears alive but signifies death; the mound appears dead but signifies life.

The plant is surrounded by an eight-foot-high fence topped with coils of barbed wire, sharp slivers of wire wrapped round in rolls mocking the sweep of waves, the living and dying surf of the ocean. The fence signals its intention despite the lack of advertising at the plant entrance that this is an industry of death: keep out, private, secret. The sharp silver wire circling the plant both attracts and repels us. It warns us that this plant is ours, that it is valuable enough to be so enclosed; at the same time it says, "Enter at your peril." It is ours and it is not.

We have paid for it just as we will pay for the savings and loan debts that the politicians left us with. The barbed wire says, "This is yours." But it proclaims its message from a distance. We cannot enter. This is private property with a public meaning, or it is public property with a private meaning. I don't think we will know which. But the meaning is a story belonging to all of us but whose telling we have been denied the chance to participate in. The story the atomic plant tells is like the ones we all learned at school. We only get to receive the story; we come passive before it. The story is universal, and it is majestically deadly. The barbed wire becomes the regal crown of a king we have consented to have rule over us. There is also a fence around the mound, apparently put up less than thirty years ago. A man I meet at the top of the mound tells me that there was no fence here when he visited as a young man. I don't remember it from my childhood visits. The fence is rusted. The cement that the posts sit in its cracked, small pieces pushed up by frosts, bits and pieces washed out by the rains. All the folly of long-term storage of nuclear wastes is revealed by this pitiful fence circling the base of the mound and running along the stone steps leading from the base to the summit. Even the stones are cracked and split. Even the stones give way before the half-life of the radioactive wastes produced by the plant.

The ice is melting on the stone steps, the frost already out of the ground reminding me that the earth of this mound is alive. Across the atomic processing plant a warm breeze blows out of the west. I am struck by the fragility of objects made of metal and wood and cement. Why can we not meditate upon the delicate nature of what appears solid long enough so that the folly of atomic war and atomic energy becomes obvious? Perhaps we have no sense of the distant death because we have no sense of what is immediately alive to us.

Beneath my feet the water table rises and falls, shifting and slipping with the earth's movement through space with the pull from planners and stars too distant to see by any telescope. Minuscule particles of plutonium and tritium ride the tides of minute ocean currents. The honey bee is seeking the flowers' pollen. The sound of crows. Roots of the grasses, bushes, and trees push out through dirt particles seeking food and water. Patches of moss grow in between the stones displacing mortar.

I remember asking my father why he was always writing notes to himself, always writing things down. And he said it was to keep his memory free. He didn't want to clutter his mind with things he could keep on paper. And I look out at the atomic weapons processing plant at the acres and acres of prosperity linked so intimately with massive, would-wide death. All those local jobs based upon distant death.

It would have been impossible for those who built this mound to comprehend death at a distance, massive death across space and time. The Adena apparently were peaceful folk. There is no evidence in the mounds of persons dying violently. No projectile points embedded in bone. If they warred they may have warred like some other Indians did; in the midst of battle they touch the enemy. They count coup. To be touched when the war attempts to distance us from each other, that can be a humiliation. It can also be the beginning of wisdom, a participatory realization of "the knowledge that connects." It is with most extreme difficulty, perhaps it is impossible, that we image it, but before the European invasion there was no such thing as death at a distance.

In his foreword to Alan Bleakley's *Fruits of the Moon Tree*, Peter Redgrove speaks to the importance of touch and its relation to how distant the western world has become to what matters: "Becoming an individual in touch with the world is what magic is all about; or, in Jungian psychology, individuation; and it is the Black Goddess who presides over individuation." The mounds offer an approach to and an appreciation for this Black Goddess, at least that is my guiding intuition about them.

The dis-ease of language, this disguise of meaning, this language used by those who advertise us out, infects us not just for the money it makes its creators but in order to create of us an image of the ideal consumer who accepts all images to keep from finding out the truth of what is behind that barbed wire. Language is used to overload our senses so we cannot see, so that we remain unaware, ill-informed. Language is used to overload us with trivia, too much information of the wrong kind.

I wonder about my father and what he did keep in memory. He kept books and magazines out of the house when my sister and I were kids. He said he didn't need to read to us; he could tell us stories that were better than those in the books, those written by someone we did not know, would never know, someone not related except through the purchase of the product. He told us stories. I remember almost nothing of them, but I still feel the presence of him when I lie in bed thinking of the telling of the stories. I felt it when I told my own children stories. I remember only that in one of the stories, or perhaps they were all linked together, perhaps it was all one long ongoing tale, I remember a quest through a forest, a trail leading to a mountain where the treasure lay buried.

The memory of my father fades. I see that the mounds themselves are stories.

The mounds are talking out of themselves so that we may learn how to talk. The mounds are true out-lines. They are suggestions, possibilities. They are ghosts, offering the possibilities for ghost writers such as myself. They are possible lines connecting us to them to the past and to each other. They are lines of force, like the force of making love, which is also making death.

The lines connecting the mounds are song lines like those recorded by Bruce Chatwin in Australia. They map the land through story. Looking west from this mound you see distant hills from which signal fires once blazed in the night. A line of fire connected this mound on the Great Miami River to the Ohio River fifty miles to the south. I think of the words *Signal and Fire*. I waver in my resolve to see the connections. The weapons plant rises before me, and the missiles are released. Mushroom clouds of misery and dying sprout in my imagination.

At one time this mound supported no vegetation. It was packed with sterile earth dug from below the living loam. As it was constructed the earth was not spilled about the growing mound, it was dumped, packed, patted, perhaps smoothed and stroked like a loving man might do the belly of a pregnant woman to touch the child growing within. There were no trees, bushes, grass. In time plants grew, perhaps waste plants like the *Datura* which sprout up in this climate anytime the earth is disturbed and which native peoples still use for ceremonial intoxication. Eventually the people must have allowed plants to root to keep the mound from eroding. But I imagine that for a long time they kept the surface bare of vegetation so that the mound stood out from the landscape.

Alan Bleakley offers a suggestion of why these mounds might have remained bald. During his journey to discover meaning in the neolithic burial chambers, he speculates about the Cornish word *mulfra*, meaning "bald hill." It is related to the Sanskrit, *mundra* "baldness" and the Latin *mundras*, "world." Certainly all of those word connections connect me to these mounds, but I am so intrigued by the other meaning of *mulfra*: "hill of clotted blood."

I am convinced as Bleakley is of the prehistoric burial chambers of England that these mounds are receptacles of female wisdom. They are true monuments but not to death as the archaeologists insist. Since the Adena built these mounds as burials, the scholars call them Mounds for the Dead. They are not. They are for the living. They are embodies stories. They are a form of writing. They make permanent things that might otherwise clutter the mind.

Archaeologists have assembled some evidence suggesting how the Adena built the mounds. There was a death, a burial of the body in an open grave with elevated sides, often open to the east, made on the floor of the house itself. A wooded structure was constructed over it with the body open to the air, perhaps laying there for a year or more. Then later the bones were removed, perhaps painted red and adorned with copper, then arranged in a variety of ways and sprinkled over with red ocher powder. A log cover was placed over them and earth piled over that. The community ceremoniously burned down the house over the earth and mounded it over again.

The resulting earth structure is not thereby a monument to death. The earth holds the memory of stories told by the communal breath of life. Imagine the soul of the dead being aided on its journey with the stories of the community. The fire sends the spirit upward. The community does not hide from death. The young sit atop the mounds to catch the spirit of the departing souls which become infused with living and the living become intoxicated with the released spirit of their community. The earth holds the memory of the community in place to be revived again, added to, changed as necessary, built upon. The mound must have been a place of story and meditation, a place of celebration.

Each mound, and over ten thousand were scattered throughout Ohio, became a point of solidity, a focus of ceremonies, and a locus for the communities. The Adena literally made a self-contained story by scraping up their villages to construct the mounds, recycling the midden, their wastes, and their history. The mound buries not any one individual but the community, enabling the community to tell another story while it remembers the story told to connect the community with its past and point it to its future. They build, live, die, walk on to build again. In so doing the whole land is marked, not just with points but with the lines connecting them. And these connections are group language; they are songs. As Chatwin says it,

> In Aboriginal belief, an unsung land is a dead land;
> since, if the songs are forgotten, the land itself
> will die. To allow that to happen was the worst of
> all possible crimes...

It becomes more and more obvious to me that the message of this mound is not just its juxtaposition to the atomic weapons plant. It is not just the life of the mound, its simplicity, its endurance over the past 2500 years or more compared to the factory of death, its complex connections with the life and language of our time, its essential fragility. The message of these mounds is more personal. The message speaks to my own survival, my own struggles to find a way of living that does not lead to the atomic weapons processing plant. These mounds contain my story, otherwise I would not be here.

* * *

WORKS CITED:
Bleakey, Alan. *Fruits of the Moon Tree*. Bath, England: 1988.
Bosnak, Rovert. *A Little Course in Dreams*. Boston: 1988.
Chatwin, Bruce. *The Songlines*. New York: 1987.

Foggy Winter morning ©*Becky Linhardt*

CLAUDE CLAYTON SMITH

CLAUDE CLAYTON SMITH is a professor of English at Ohio Northern University in Ada, Ohio, where he lives with his wife and two sons. He is the author of four books plus a variety of fiction, poetry, essays and reviews. His work has been translated into five languages. "Hardin County Ditch Watch" is from a series of articles he is doing on the "Ohio outback." The essay appeared as "Ditch Watch" in the February 1993 edition of *Ohio Magazine*.

Robert Frost wrote, "Something there is that doesn't love a wall." Or a ditch, Claude Clayton Smith might add. In "Hardin County Ditch Watch," Smith writes that "life comes and goes along the county ditches…" In particular, Smith trains his eye(s) on the ditches that run alongside Hardin County Road 50 near Ada, Ohio. Mixing anecdotes with facts, Smith brings the ditches to life by showing the life they attract: from the animals and plants that inhabit them to the man who mows them, to the neighbors who live alongside them, to the unfortunate drivers who have had mishaps because of them.

HARDIN COUNTY DITCH WATCH

Hardin County Road 50 begins in rural farmland two and a half miles east of the village of Ada and runs due west to the county line six miles away. The middle mile of this straight stretch—a residential section bisected by State Route 235 (Main Street, Ada)—is known as Lima Avenue and falls under the jurisdiction of the village. Here the speed limit drops to 35 m.p.h., but on CR 50, to the east and west, there are no signs and the local traffic is fast.

East of Ada CR 50 is oppressively flat, but to the west—where I live—it rolls a bit, cresting and dipping three times before it reaches the county line, so that oncoming cars are momentarily hidden. The surrounding farmland, interrupted by occasional woodlots, is seasonally devoted to corn, soybeans and winter wheat. On the whole, the countryside appears much the way it did to those who settled the area a century and a half ago.

Grassy drainage ditches accompany CR 50 the entire length of its run. They measure 10 feet wide from the edge of the road and range in depth from a few inches to as much as seven feet. At their shallowest they have the contour of a check mark; at their deepest they are more nearly V-shaped. Channeled at intervals beneath the road, these ditches join larger waterways that run north to Hog "Crick" and Grass Run outside of Ada, then west to the Ottawa River, which continues north and west to the Maumee. In theory, and with a lot of luck, a toy boat placed in the ditch along CR 50 could make it all the way to Lake Erie. Or you could skate there after a deep freeze.

If a man's home is his castle, then his ditch is his moat, especially after a heavy rain. Not that we need to defend our privacy out here in the country. There are only 14 homes strung out along the final two miles of CR 50, set back from the ditches on plots of one to five acres with nothing but farmland for a backyard. Most were built since the '60s, although a few go back to the turn of the century. Two have been replaced after burning to the ground, at a time when water in the ditch might have helped the volunteer firemen.

But on the day we moved in, our ditch was an enemy. It was 35 degrees and drizzling, the water running ankle deep through a galvanized pipe beneath the gravel driveway. The neck of the drive is only 18 feet wide—the same width as the paved surface of CR 50—and the movers spent half an hour backing the van in, trying to avoid the ditch to either side as well as the parallel ditch on the north side of the road. The ruts they left in the lawn are still visible, an ugly reminder of the wet spring of 1989.

Later that day our attention was drawn to a utility pole at the back of the ditch across the street. A large red squirrel had chewed through the power line, electrocuting itself and setting the top of the pole ablaze. A neighbor called the power company—our telephone was not yet hooked up—and a truck was dispatched from United Rural Electric. By the time it arrived the pole looked like the Olympic torch and the air was thick with the stench of burnt fur. Undaunted, the lineman stepped into the ditch, filled his yellow hard hat with water, and steered himself aloft in a "cherry picker" to douse the flames. Then he knocked the blackened carcass of the squirrel into the ditch.

That night the temperature dipped below freezing, and at dawn a car slid into the ditch just to the east of us, clipping off a utility pole at its base. On each of the next two mornings there were crumpled cars off the road at the same spot, and I realized that these country ditches were to be reckoned with.

A friend from Wood County tells me that folks out his way routinely burn their ditches, to stunt the scrub brush and facilitate the drainage—everybody standing along the roadside leaning on rakes, the ditches ablaze and smoking for miles. At Ohio Northern University in Ada I met a student whose uncle, David Aller, is one of the few people certified to burn ditches in Hancock County. He does it as a sideline and apparently it's quite an art. Most of his work is at intersections and near corners where the wild growth obscures the traffic. But I've never seen the ditches afire along CR 50. The farmers, homeowners and Hardin County personnel keep them relatively free of vegetation, although thorny locusts tend to establish themselves readily, escaping from neighboring hedgerows and windbreaks.

Hardin County assistant engineer Mike Smith says that CR 50 is resurfaced with a two inch cold mix every 10 years or so and receives a chip-and-seal treatment on a two year cycle after that. The ditches, however, get more attention. Seven times a year—May 10 through the end of October—county employee Bob Leis cuts the grass along the right-of-way on CR 50, between the edge of the road and the telephone poles. He uses a John Deere diesel tractor with a 10 foot cutting arm and a five foot wide flail behind. The tractor's two front tires are about the size of those on a pickup truck, but the two rear tubeless tires stand five feet tall.

Keeping the left wheel on the berm and the right wheel in the grass of the ditch, Leis makes sure that his first cut is not too severe. It's on his second pass that the debris turns up. Then the flail goes to work—a heavy roller containing 36 knife blades covered by a metal shell—pulverizing the bottles, beer cans and other trash. Leis gets fewer flat tires from broken glass these days—about three a summer—because the front tractor tires now have a foam which seals off punctures.

Since the grass is thick and tough in the spring, Leis can make only one pass with the tractor on his first time out. A few years ago, in an effort to protect the pheasants and other birds that nest in the ditches, the State of Ohio required all mowers to make but a single pass until mid-July, when the birds come up and take cover among the crops in the field. The strategy seems to be working. Leis saw more pheasants this past summer than in previous years. I have seen them, too— a bonus of my daily ditch watch—on afternoon jogs to the county line and back, and Bob Leis was glad to hear it.

Often while mowing Leis has to raise the cutting bar on his tractor to avoid hitting snakes, baby raccoons and other living creatures in the ditch. Cats are the biggest problem—they wait until the last second to move away. He's afraid he'll cut off their legs. Dogs are a problem, too. Running out from the neighboring yards to bark at the tractor, they put themselves in danger of the traffic, so Leis has to stop work and get their owners after them. He sees a lot of *dead* dogs and cats, too. "People just throw 'em in the ditch," he says. "To get rid of 'em."

Once, Leis hit a skunk and went stinking for a week. On another occasion, when the rear wheels of his tractor crunched a six-pack, he got squirted with beer and returned to the garage smelling like a drunk. But sometimes he gets lucky, as when five dollars came rolling up out of the ditch one day, sticking to the tractor wheel—the only money he's found in ten years on the job. The biggest danger he faces is turning over, because the ditch occasionally drops off sharply, leaving the tractor riding at steep angles, but he likes the challenge and has never rolled his machine. His greatest fear is people—he's afraid of getting slammed by drunks on the road—yet most people, he concedes, are pretty courteous. When it's foggy, he simply doesn't mow. Occasionally, the farmers will get after him about cutting too close to their crops, but in general the complaints are few. All in all, to hear Bob Leis tell it, there are worse jobs than mowing the ditches in Hardin County.

For those of us who live along CR 50 and subscribe to the *Lima News*, the ditches out front pose a challenge of a different sort. Not so if you take the *Kenton Times*, because the *Times* supplies its customers with a blue-and-white monogrammed receptacle that can be attached to the post of your mailbox. But the *Lima News* is flung from the window of a passing vehicle that barely slows to 50 m.p.h.. The paper is rolled and secured with an elastic band which often breaks on impact, scattering the paper along the ditch. In wet weather it comes in a thin blue plastic wrapper, but even that can get chewed up enough as it hits the gravel driveway so that the paper explodes and blows away. Or if it lands in the ditch—either short of the driveway or beyond it—water seeps in through the open end of the wrapper, making the paper unreadable. Often I've had to purchase another at the Dairy Mart in Ada because ours got destroyed in delivery. But if the paper were put in our mailbox, it would take the carrier twice as long to do the route and cost twice as much in gasoline, what with all the stopping and starting. Such is the price—to carrier and customer—of country living with a ditch by the side of the road.

Not long after hunting for the *Lima News* became part of my daily ditch watch, something happened to put that problem in perspective. One Saturday night in May of 1989, an Ada man and a Lafayette woman heading west on CR 50 plowed through the ditch about a mile to the west of us and struck a tree at the edge of the woodlot there. Neither was wearing a seatbelt and the man was killed. The woman, who was driving, explained that the car had gone off the edge of the road to the right, then swerved back across and into the woods. The ditches at that point fall away immediately to a depth of three feet, so disaster was waiting on either side. Had the car continued to the right, it would have rolled several times into the fields. A year later, on the anniversary of the accident, a white wooden cross and a spray of plastic flowers were placed in the ditch at the base of the fatal tree. In the interval I noticed mute evidence of other mishaps that might have proved just as tragic— black skid marks veering toward the ditches in summer, muddy ruts through the ditches in winter, all coming to an abrupt and chilling halt.

It's a wonder more people haven't been killed, especially where CR 50 reaches CR 15, the county line road. CR 50 should come to an end there, forcing motorists to stop and turn north or south. But the road cuts sharply to the left for 10 yards or so, creating a wide and dangerous intersection, before heading due west again toward Lima as the Lafayette Road. Cars coming east at that point often end up in the fields on the south side of the road, unable to negotiate the quick turn. Last January, after a stretch of foggy weather produced numerous tire tracks in the fields, three small metal reflectors were installed on stakes at the end of CR 50, to catch the headlights of motorists coming out of Allen County. In February I found the first of those stakes flat against the earth and straddled by muddy tire tracks, a wheel cover lying nearby. In March the other two were leveled. In the fall of 1992 yellow lines were painted down the center of County Road 50, but drivers tend to ignore them. By defining lanes, the lines seem to narrow the distance to the ditches.

Dale Badertscher, who farms 220 acres along CR 50, has pulled his share of vehicles out of the ditches and fields by the county line over the years. At one point, when the land he rents was fenced in for cattle, eastbound cars used to miss that sharp turn at least once a month. He was always chasing cattle and repairing the fence. Last winter I asked him about a set of deep tracks that ran through the ditch into the field to the north of the road, missing a utility pole by three feet. He said that a neighbor had heard the car, and the driver was "going faster than he should have." Which is usually the case.

Badertscher has been farming the land along CR 50 for the last 18 years, and for seven years before that with his father. He's got a collection of more than 100 arrowheads that he's found in the fields as he works. And counted among his souvenirs is a green Coke bottle that turned up one day when his plow caught a piece of the ditch. "When's the last time you saw a Coke bottle like that?" he asks. Like Bob Leis, he gets a few flat tires each season from glass bottles in the field. In the old days bottles and cans would hurt the combine, but the newer equipment, he says, just "chops 'em up and spits 'em back." Any debris that gets into the grain is cleaned in the processing. And like Leis he has found a few dollar bills on the job. Yet his most precious find has proved priceless—a puppy, part Husky, that was abandoned in the ditch just after weaning. The dog, named "Tippy" for its white-tipped tail, has been a part of the Badertscher family for 11 years now.

During the course of last winter I noticed many tracks through the ditches on my daily jog to the county line and back. They always seem to be made after dark, and they all occur in the final mile of CR 50, where there are only two houses— a new ranch owned by Richard Klingler on the north side of the road and an old farm house, no longer occupied, just opposite, in front of the big red barn and outbuildings that are very much in use and bear the name of Warren and Zelma Lacey. These buildings lie just to the west of the intersection of CR 50 and St. Paul Road (Liberty Twp. 15), and from there, once you pass the woodlot that claimed the life of the Ada man, it's an open roller-coaster ride to the county line.

The scariest tracks, left by two vehicles, appeared in front of the Klingler place after a snow storm, one set tearing up his lawn and the other knocking out the chain link fence in front of the empty farm house across the street—as if approaching cars had swerved through the ditches to avoid a head-on collision. A few days later, after the February ice storm which caused so many accidents throughout the state, I traced a curious and continuous set of tracks through the field just to the east of Richard Klingler's home. A vehicle, heading west, had cut through the ditch at the intersection of St. Paul Road, run parallel to CR 50 for several hundred yards, then cut back through the ditch to the road again. The storm had caused a whiteout and perhaps the driver had lost his way. Or maybe the maneuver had been done on purpose, since drifting snow was closing the roads. I would have felt more comfortable about those tracks in the field had the driver not emerged from the ditch so close to a utility pole.

Bob Allen, Jr., who grew up in the farmhouse across the street from us, has a whiteout story with a happier ending. It was 1935 and Allen, later mayor of Ada, was in the first grade. School was let out early—about 2:00 P.M.—because of a winter storm. The temperature was minus 30, the snow was blowing and drifting, and the visibility was zero. The school bus came to a halt on St. Paul Road and could go no further, so Allen and a dozen other children were let off to walk home. The first boy out stepped into the ditch and sank waist-high in snow. Then the bigger kids carried the smaller kids across the fields, where the snow wasn't as deep, to Paul Klingler's place. But the Klinglers had no phone. Back on CR 50, Allen's parents were beginning to worry. His mother Falita, who passed away last year, was pregnant at the time and had a broken leg to boot. When darkness fell, his father—the late Robert Allen, Sr.—set out west along CR 50 to Isaiah Klingler's, the only home in the area with a telephone. It was only a quarter of a mile away, but he almost didn't make it, falling down several times, hunched over into the teeth of the wind, making his way along a fence at the back of the ditch. At Isaiah's place he learned that the kids were all safe at Paul's, but it was 9:00 P.M. before he could get back to tell his wife. The children—enjoying the holiday—returned home the next day on horse-drawn sleds.

The Allen homestead sits across the street from us on several acres of land that are screened from view on CR 50 by a row of junipers along the back of the ditch. The bushes, 10 feet tall and six feet deep, run for 75 yards from the east corner of the property to the gravel driveway in the middle of the lot. Beyond the driveway, however, they continue only another six yards. I once asked Falita Allen what happened to the rest of the row.

Well, she said, one afternoon a few years ago they heard a strange noise out front. A car heading towards Ada had gone off the road, cut across the ditch and mowed down the junipers, leaving it on top of the bushes, wheels spinning. The driver, a young man in his early 20s, climbed down and wandered into the house to use the telephone, but Robert Allen, Sr. asked him to leave, since the man was obviously drunk or on drugs. The car had to be pulled off the junipers with a backhoe. Meanwhile, the driver disappeared. Later that evening Fred Lissner, who lives to the west of the Allen property beyond a large field, saw a light on in his car outside. The door was open. Someone had been fooling with the car. Then *his* neighbor across the street reported a car missing. The keys had been in it. Police traced the license of the car on the junipers and found the young man who had stolen the neighbor's car. The Allens replaced the bushes with some other small shrubs, but the huge gap in the row is still very much evident.

A more stately landmark on the Allen property stands among the junipers just to the east of the driveway—one of the largest oak trees in Hardin County. The tree is so huge that if you stand right up against its trunk and spread your arms wide, anyone standing beyond the tree can't see your fingertips. The branches—thick and gnarled—overhang the ditches on both sides of the road. Bob Allen says that that tree was enormous when *he* was a kid, and when people like the Klinglers were settling the area in the 1800s they used to have picnics in the shade of its branches. "When you live in a place," he says, reminiscing, "you don't realize it's a part of history."

Many members of the Klingler family are buried in the country graveyard on St. Paul Road, where the tombstones date to the Civil War. And some of the marble slabs there—especially those that face west—go back much earlier, the inscriptions rubbed smooth by the wind and rain. Anna Belle Klingler, who is in her seventies, is the mother of Richard Klingler and the widow of Keith Klingler, who went to school with Falita and Robert Allen, Sr. She's been in the area for 60 years and has lived on CR 50—where Isaiah Klingler used to live—since 1953, last home to the west of us before St. Paul Road. She can recall when there was only one house between herself and Ada. The house she lives in was built in the '40s to replace the one that burned down, "a big old 16 room farmhouse that had runnin' water and a bathroom when no one else did." The furnace just exploded one October—stove pipe combustion due to an accumulation of dust in the registers—when her mother-in-law went to start it up for the winter. "And that," Anna Belle laughs, "was the first and last fire of the year."

Anna Belle, whose mother was Mary Belle, owns the land that Dale Badertscher farms. She says that all the neighborhood farmers worked together to get a waterway put in, laying drainage tiles in their fields to get the water to the roadside ditches and beyond. Her son Richard owns the Lacey farm across from his ranch house down the road, but he's not a farmer. He works for a Japanese firm in Bluffton because, as Anna Belle says, "You don't get rich on a farm."

Between Main Street, Ada, and the county line road, CR 50 is intersected only twice—by St. Paul Road to the west of us and Liberty Township 35, known as "Klingler Road," to the east, each one mile apart. According to Anna Belle, the Klinglers came to America from Germany in the early 19th century, but it's impossible to keep them all straight. A family tree made in 1910 dates back to an Amos Klingler, who had six or seven sons and one daughter, and to Amos' father, who had 18 children, before that. The original family tree has been lost, but Sam Klingler had copies made up for a family reunion a few years ago. He was 100 years old at the time.

"Now you take the Lacey farm," Anna Belle says. "Warren and Zelma were brother and sister. His grandma and my husband's father were first cousins. Warren was married once, but his wife run him off with a butcher knife. When he passed away he left the place to Zelma, who died an old maid a few years ago, at the age of 97."

Fred Lissner, who lives across the way from Anna Belle, jogs daily along CR 50 like myself, except he's been doing it longer—more than 13 years now—and he goes further, a mile or two into Allen County on the Lafayette Road, before turning back. He says he used to see an old lady sitting on the porch at the Lacey place—that would have been Zelma—and he'd wave and cross to the far side of the road so as not to frighten her. The Lissners live in a ranch house built to replace their Victorian style clapboard farmhouse that burned down in 1982. They had gone to Lima one Sunday afternoon and when they returned their old house—which used to sit just 30 feet back from the ditch—was a pile of blackened rubble. The cause was never determined. For a few weeks after that they lived where we do now, while the previous owner was out of town.

Fred Lissner agrees that jogging along CR 50 can be dangerous. You have to run facing the traffic. As I mentioned earlier, the paved surface is only 18 feet wide and the ditches slope away immediately. American vehicles average six feet in width, and if cars coming from each direction keep a three foot berth between them, that leaves only 18 inches along the roadside for joggers. "The old folks don't really see you," Lissner says, "so you have to get the hell out of the way." Fortunately, the local traffic is light, even in the late afternoon when I usually pass Lissner somewhere along CR 50. It takes me 30 minutes to get to the county line and back, and in that time I won't encounter but half a dozen vehicles. Like Lissner, however, I often step down into the ditch when I hear them coming.

Lissner has seen every kind of animal, dead and alive, along the road and in the ditches over the years—dogs, cats, groundhogs, deer, possum, raccoons, snakes, skunks—he's even been chased by a flock of birds. "I'm not too sure they didn't want to attack me," he says. In the warmer months, the crows and turkey vultures take care of the road kill, posting their sentinels in the trees of the woodlots and persistently pecking at the carrion, despite an occasional jogger or car. In the colder months the carcasses eventually get knocked into the ditches, or the injured animals crawl in there to die.

In some of the fields along CR 50 cows graze right up to the fence at the back of the ditch. "They like to get up and talk to me," Lissner says. Sometimes the entire herd will begin to jog along with him. Like Bob Leis and Dale Badertscher, he has found a bit of cash along CR 50, but unlike me he doesn't concentrate on the ditches—he likes to listen for the whistles of the trains that run parallel to CR 50 in the fields to the north, counting the boxcars or looking for passengers in the Amtrak, trying to beat them to the next intersection.

The only other afternoon jogger that goes as far as the county line and back is John Magee of Ada, who has been running the route since 1976. Magee remembers the day the Lissner's house burned down. He had seen Fred and his wife leaving for Lima as he jogged by, and later, as he was getting into the bathtub after his run, he heard sirens and could see smoke to the west. Apparently, the house had been on fire as he passed it on his way back to Ada.

The Lissners had a determined hound dog that used to climb out of its pen—right over a fence topped with barbed wire—and chase Magee as he jogged by. But one day as it came barking across the yard, Magee heard a car approaching from behind, and the dog was struck and killed as it emerged from the roadside ditch.

Like the others who pass the ditches daily, Magee has found some money along CR 50—three dollar bills, one after another, just laying there waiting to be picked up. But a surprise of a different sort awaited him one day, the kind that reflects the wanton freedom generated by an open country road. Not far from the county line on the south side of CR 50 there used to be a large tree in the ditch. You can still see its stump. One afternoon as Magee jogged by, two young men were sitting in the ditch in the shade of that tree, smoking dope. "They asked me to join them," he says. The fields were green and the day was warm, but Magee continued on his way—beneath white clouds and a wide blue sky—on a "high" of his own.

Everybody I've talked with about the ditches along CR 50 has found money there, except me. And yet I observe the ditches daily. Once, when my wife and I were biking along with our two boys, our older son slammed on his brakes and skidded to a halt at what appeared to be a twenty dollar bill in the grass at the edge of the ditch. But it was only "funny money," and we all felt cheated—victims of a practical joke in the middle of nowhere.

Then one November, quite suddenly, the ditches along CR 50 became a gold mine. A letter from Brown Refuse, which collects our trash, asked us to begin separating our garbage for recycling. This led me to look at the ditches in a new way. In the months since moving in I hadn't really noticed the litter on my daily jog—the beer cans, the bottles, the paper—but all at once that was all I saw.

On a whim I looked up "litter" in the card catalogue at the ONU library in Ada. There was only one entry—*Litter: The Ugly Enemy*, a nonfiction book for young adults by Dorothy E. Shuttlesworth. Published in 1973, it describes what citizens can do to clean up their communities and launch consciousness-raising campaigns against litter.

A good idea, I thought, to educate the young, but why weren't there more entries? I tried the *Reader's Guide to Periodical Literature* but found only "cat litter." Then, under "pollution," I hit the jackpot—acid rain, air pollution, chemical plants, medical waste, pesticides, radioactive waste, radon, space debris, trade waste, etc.—everything but beer cans and bottles. Compared to the rest of the environment, I guess, the ditches of Ohio are in pretty good shape. Old fashioned litter has become a quaint item, yet it remains a very big problem, and because of it my ditch watch is turning a profit.

Inspired by the request from Brown Refuse, I began to pick up aluminum cans from the ditches on my daily jog to the county line and back, stomping them flat and putting them in a plastic bag or tucking them into the pocket of my windbreaker. In the first six months I collected 540 cans, which—at 28 cents per pound—is worth $6.00 at the Ice Plant Recycling Center in Ada. Based on those figures, I project an annual income of $12.00, seven dollars more than Bob Leis has found in 12 years of mowing the ditches in Hardin County.

Most of the cans are beer cans, with an occasional pop container. I don't pick up bottles—they're too heavy and dangerous. They're also not as plentiful. An inventory I took one January day revealed a total of 84 glass bottles—pop bottles, beer bottles, wine bottles and liquor bottles—in the ditches between here and the county line. The number remains fairly constant, and I assume that this glass will eventually get crushed during the summer months by the flail on Bob Leis's tractor.

I used to think that littering was an unconscious act, but the evidence in the ditches proves otherwise. I often find, for example, a half dozen or more beer cans jettisoned in a cardboard 12-pack container. Nearly every pop bottle I have seen has its cap on, the peeled labels often tucked inside. Several bags of trash that I've examined—from area fast food chains—contained, along with french fries packets and soft drink cups, a pile of cigarette butts from a dashboard ashtray.

The littering is constant. I average three cans a day, and can't remember the last time I came home empty handed. And the litterers are by and large the same people. Every week or so I collect several blue and beige Schaefer Light cans that have been crushed in an identical manner—end to end like an accordion—before they are thrown out. Generally, I find more cans on Saturday and Sunday than during the week. And almost all of the littering occurs—like the accidents and tire tracks—in the last open mile before the county line. The time of year makes no difference. I've picked up beer cans on Thanksgiving, Christmas and Easter. People who litter do not take holidays.

Ordinance 521.08 of the Ada Health, Safety and Welfare Code governs "littering and the deposit of garbage, rubbish, junk, etc." Technically, bottles and cans are "rubbish" and littering is a misdemeanor, punishable by a $100 fine. The Ohio Revised Code, which applies to both state and county jurisdictions, contains the same language, except that the court costs and fines are a little higher. Unfortunately, those laws are rarely enforced.

I asked Anne Boston, program manager at the Hardin County Office of Litter Prevention and Recycling, about littering in the ditches in Hardin County. She recalls an incident in an area near CR 50 where a road was closed for bridge repairs. From the ditch there county workers removed a refrigerator, three tires, pieces of concrete and brick, seven bags of trash, and a stack of old license plates. The plates were traced to an individual who had hired someone to dump the load. The offender paid a $250 fine plus court costs, was placed on probation for a year, and had to perform four days of public service.

Anne Boston sent me the Hardin County litter crew records for 1988 and 1989. They indicate which county roads were cleaned and how many bags of trash were picked up. CR 50 was not listed. This leads me to believe that our road is cleaner than most, since only roads specified by the supervisor get attention. The records detail the area covered, the date, the man hours, the miles covered on foot, and the bags of litter collected. The crew, which only works from May to October, shares in the recycling profits from what it collects. The workers average three bags of litter per mile. If I were to pick up all the trash I see in the mile and a half between my home and the county line, I estimate it would fill less than one bag, so I can understand why CR 50 hasn't been policed by the county in recent years.

Most of the paper I see in the ditches either blows away or breaks apart after a rain. Much of it, besides the fast food bags, consists of cigarette wrappers. Then there is the automobile junk—wheel covers, fan belts, exhaust pipes, and metal door strips. This stuff isn't littered but simply falls from passing vehicles, although empty oil containers and jugs of windshield fluid are often tossed into the ditches on purpose. It gets discouraging, despite the relative cleanliness of CR 50. But there is hope. Ohio House Bill 592 has set a goal for Ohioans to recycle 25 percent of all garbage in our waste stream by 1994. That's a start, and the recycling habit—as I've found—can become infectious as well as profitable.

But my recycling effort by no means dominates my ditch watch. I enjoy talking to folks along CR 50. And every season out here brings special moments. Wildflowers dot the ditches in summer. In the fall, leaves from the Allen's big oak fill our ditch and my boys dive into them. In winter, ditch water flows through the untouched snowdrifts like a black brush stroke. One spring I monitored a robin's nest—in a locust thicket in the ditch between the Allens' and the Lissners'. Each day as I approached, the four chicks within would close their gaping beaks and rotate downward in unison into a feathery ball. The mother robin would wait until I had jogged on by before bringing her worm to the nest. Later, using binoculars from beyond the ditch across the street, I watched two of the four make their first flights into the cornfield beyond. Their abandoned nest is still in the thicket, a reminder that life comes and goes along the county ditches, and always has.

Lake Erie shoreline in Vermilion ©Dennis Horan

ROBERT FLANAGAN

ROBERT FLANAGAN has published a novel, *Maggot*, and two collections of stories, *Naked to Naked Goes* and *Loving Power*. His stories have been published in *Chicago*, *Fiction*, *Ohio Review* and *Kansas Quarterly*. In addition, he has authored two stage plays and a comedy screenplay, *Teller's Ticket*, which was produced in Columbus, Ohio in 1989 and won first place in The Hometown USA Video Festival in Oregon. As a poet, Flanagan has published five chapbooks of poems in the U.S., Canada and Ireland. His work appears in a number of anthologies, most recently in *The Norton Anthology of Short Fiction* and *An Introduction to Poetry*, edited by X.J. Kennedy. Flanagan lives in Delaware, Ohio, where he is Director of Creative Writing at Ohio Wesleyan University.

Like so many other essays in this collection, "Life's Fiction, Fiction's Life" is about the influences on a person's life that played a part in his becoming a writer. Flanagan tells of growing up in the working class world of Toledo, Ohio, "The Glass Center of the World," located in the northwestern part of the state, and introduces us to the people who helped to form his individual character—and who later became his fictional characters. As reflective writing often is, this essay is based on a simple question: How did I come to be?

LIFE'S FICTION, FICTION'S LIFE

Attention

Writing is a matter of attention. At the simplest level this means getting attention. Like children, writers want people to notice them. Look, look at what I made!

The people in my family were talkers. Their lives pared down by hard times, they entertained themselves by playing word games, mocking their supposed betters with sly jokes, and recounting past family exploits to a point that they took on mythic status. If you wanted to hold your own at those late night boozy kitchen table confabs, you had to know how to tell a story. When you had judged your listeners' interest and patience correctly, dropping the punch line at just the right moment, your reward was a burst of laughter. And family pride. An uncle might clap you on the shoulder and compliment your grinning father, "Red, this kid's no dummy."

At a deeper level writing is a way of paying attention to the world. Translating the coded messages behind the slogans we live by is hard work that requires conditioning the self to be acutely and painfully conscious.

As a boy in Catholic schools I was forever being told to "Pay Attention." It seemed that frequently I would float off somewhere in my head. At the end of my teens I was called to attention—"Ten-hut!"—in the Marines. There, the veil of familiarity stripped from things, I began to take notice, and to question.

At still another level writing is a way of deflecting attention from the performing self onto the subject. In fiction, since subject matter most often is character, this may mean calling attention to others.

When I was younger I wrote to escape my reality and to parade my talent. Sinking deeper into fiction over the years, I became less concerned with self-display and more interested in calling attention to those who commonly go unnoticed by society. "Attention must be paid to such a man," I'd say, quoting Miller, although it was my father's fate, not Willy Loman's, that spurred me to work.

Writing holds surprising rewards. The act of creation which spirits you away from family and community may in time return you to them as you learn to pay better attention to things beyond the self. But there are costs as well. Fiction that aims at truth is very demanding of the writer. It calls everything into question. It requires a balancing act between the private and public self. Like the writer, it contains its opposite and is created at tension.

The Glass Center of the World

I was born and raised in the Ohio city that makes the scales used to weigh-in prizefighters ("He tipped the Toledo's at 159 and one-half"), the home of Owens-Illinois and Libby-Owens-Ford, companies that owed their success to old Mike Owens, my Dad liked to point out, an immigrant Mick who taught the high muckety-mucks a thing or two and made a bundle in doing it; the Glass Center of the World, as its billboards bragged, where the triple A ball club for a time bore the bizarre moniker "the Glass Sox;" an industrial town of workers' neat houses clustered feudally about Willys Jeep and Auto-Lite, Spitzer Paper Box and Pinkerton Tobacco, and the Champion Spark Plug plant where my mother worked as a machine operator for twenty-five years.

My father's father John and his father Thomas came to America from Aghoo village, County Roscommon, Ireland in 1890. They left behind John's sister Bridget to scrabble a living out of the eight acres that was insufficient to support them all. I don't know how long the farm had been in the family, but it was a long time. When I went to Ireland in 1978 to see the stone homestead, now tumbled and roofless and part of the Martin dairy farm, I was moved to hear the Martin brothers remark that some of their cows were up in 'Flanagan's field.' John, son of Thomas Flanagan and Honorah Mattimoe, married to Mary Cody of Hugginstown, County Kilkenny, set up residence on City Park in Saint Patrick's parish, a Toledo neighborhood crammed with Irish who kept a goat in the backyard and a bin full of potatoes in the cellar. Thomas took his shovel and got work on the streets and John joined the police force. My father, Robert, was John's second son. Hard times ended his education at the sixth grade. He went to work as a bellhop at the Boody House hotel to help his father support a family of nine on a policeman's pay. The oldest child, Mayme, had died suddenly of pneumonia, and Jim, the older son, couldn't be looked to for help; despite the Captain's frequent use of the razor strop, Jim ran with a bad crowd of cornerboys and Earl, the youngest son, was a precocious drunk. But no one worried much about Rob's missed schooling; a flame-haired bundle of energy, quick-witted, skilled at tap-dancing, acrobatics and boxing, he was a go-getter sure to make his mark in a land of opportunity.

My mother's family came from Redruth, Cornwall. Her grandfather, Samuel Treloar, was a tinsmith with an attached cottage on Foundry Row. He emigrated to Canada where he started up his own foundry. His son Charles left Canada for the States and became a traveling insurance salesman; in Georgetown, Ohio he met and married a schoolteacher, Almona Robinson. They settled on a sixty acre farm on Summerfield Road near Petersburg, Michigan, struggling to provide for their six children. Despite persistent poverty, Charles Treloar thought of himself as an aristocrat whose talents and abilities went unappreciated by his country neighbors. His youngest daughter he named Minnie, after a prosperous sister who failed to reward her brother with a monetary gift for the honor. Devilish and lively, Minnie seemed unafraid of the tyrant father the rest of the family shied from. She tried to cure his stiff neck by sneaking up behind him and giving it a sudden jerk. She substituted sand for sugar in his coffee to see if he could tell the difference. Hearing a new phrase at school one day, she skipped all the way home past neighbors' houses chanting at the top of her lungs so as not to forget it: 'Son of a bitch, son of a bitch!' Minnie began high school but collapsed with a severe case of tonsillitis. A bleeder, she was sick for months after her tonsils were removed, at times coughing up blood so thick it looked like chunks of liver. In those days, if you didn't pass the year-end tests you were charged a fee for the otherwise free schooling; the Treloars couldn't afford to pay, so upon recovery Minnie stayed at home to help her mother with housework. Resenting her father's heavy drinking and bad temper, she refused to surrender to his rule. She dropped what she felt was a rube's name, Minnie, in favor of her middle name, Jane. She shocked the family by getting her hair bobbed. Finally she packed her things, and in a new flapper dress caught the inter-urban train to Toledo where a red-headed tap dancer offered to help carry her bags.

Our family rented a one bedroom apartment on Monroe Street near Detroit Avenue. It was above Maloney's Bar & Grill, which stood between the Do-All machine shop and Ideal furniture store. "Here we are," my father would joke, "living on the far side of Ideal." He took the bedroom, my mother slept with my sister Mona Mary, ten years older than I, in the Murphy bed that pulled down from the living room closet, and my bed was against one wall of the small dining room which also held my desk and toys. Swayne Field, home of the Mud Hens, was a half block away and we could see most of the playing field from our back porch. I stood out on Detroit Avenue summer nights waiting for home run balls to sail over the right field fence.

Dad was a disabled veteran, a shell-shocked World War I U.S. Marine Corps machine gunner, one of the Devil Dogs who'd broken the German advance at Belleau Wood and Chateau Thierry. His veteran's compensation check barely paid the rent. Sometimes he held down a sort of job, part-time or short-term. When he was short order cook downstairs at Maloney's we had jumbo pickerel for supper on Fridays; he'd run it up the back stairs wrapped in his apron. But it was Mom, ten years younger than Dad and tall and wiry where he was short and stout, who supported us. Soon after I was born, when we were without light and heat due to unpaid bills, she got hired on at Champion Spark Plug as part of the World War II industrial effort. As Dad said, or I think I remember him saying, "Best thing that ever happened to this family was the Japs hitting Pearl Harbor." She worked second trick, making 5,000 aviation plugs every night, and came home about midnight five nights a week completely exhausted. I waited up for her. "Oh Laws," she would say, "I'm so tired I could just die." Dad never cracked any jokes right then, and was quick to pour her a beer. In the afternoons when he was sleeping, I sat with her at the kitchen table as she got ready for work, watching her tape her fingers to keep them from getting cut up by the freshly tooled cores. I took pride in her endurance, and in her ability to handle such demanding work. Years later when I learned how to tape my hands for boxing, making sure to pad the knuckles and to cross over to support the thumb, it was my mother I thought of, hoping I'd prove to be as brave as she was.

But this was long before it became chic for women to drive bulldozers and men to be liberated to laundry, and my dominant feeling was one of shame that my father stayed at home, jobless, while my mother headed off to the factory. At school a nun scolded me in front of our class because on the student information form in the space provided for *Father's Occupation* I had written "Housewife." She thought I was being a smart-aleck, and maybe I was. I learned early on to use a stinging wit, like a jab, to keep the nuns and my fellow parochial school inmates at a safe distance.

At times Dad crawled under the table if a car backfired in the street. When he was in the veteran's hospital at Brecksville his hands shook constantly; to drink coffee without spilling it he held one end of a towel with the fingers that gripped the cup's handle, then with the towel looped about his neck he'd tug on it with the other hand, guiding the cup to his lips. Once when he'd lost still another job he came home and locked himself in his room and plucked out his eyebrows and the front locks of his red hair. For some time after he covered his head with a white kerchief knotted at the four corners.

Rarely did I bring a friend to the apartment. I didn't want anyone to see my father walking around in his old blue robe dusting the furniture with wadded tissues or burning canned soup for our supper. Mom and Mona had jobs, so mostly it was just Dad and me at home. All the while he cooked or cleaned he was telling me, or maybe himself, stories of the heroic past. My grandfather, Captain John Flanagan, once shook hands with the great John L. Sullivan himself and was in the police cordon about the ring at the Dempsey-Willard fight, July 4, 1919 in Toledo's Bay View Park. Helping the bloodied Willard from the ring he had to beat back sore losers trying to sucker-punch the man they'd bet on. My uncle Francis Delora, Lieutenant Detective, kicked down a door in a hail of Tommy gun fire to shoot it out with the notorious Cowboy Hill.

Not very often, but sometimes, Dad talked about his own neighborhood scrapes and boxing matches, but never about the war. It was hard for me to imagine him in combat, although I'd seen for myself his Purple Heart and Presidential Citation and, in the bottom drawer of his dresser, the gas mask and the dented green helmet with a red Indian head on the front, an insignia he had painted on the helmets of his whole platoon. My father was nearly fifty when I was born, an old and broken fifty, and seemed more like my grandfather. Listening to the tales of his past, I'd try to match up the pot-bellied, skinny-armed man before me with the battler in the story. Sometimes I thought he was making it all up. Generally though I believed his story because it was so clear that he believed it. And because I wanted to believe it. I was hungry for a sense of personal history, as if that might confirm my worth, of which I was in grave doubt.

One of the things I learned at home was that though our people hadn't come up in the world, we were a damn sight more interesting and had a helluva lot better stories to tell than the bloodless types who were better off. Another thing I learned, a teaching confirmed later by church and military, was that I was special because I was part of a select unit of mankind; yet I was a very undeserving part of that unit and could be expelled.

When he wasn't talking about the grand past, Dad was whipping up visions of a wonderful future. One of us would do something to hit it big and we'd all be on easy street. I was clever, it could happen to me, I could be the one.

As a young boy I wanted to be a cowboy or a priest, a cop or a boxer. While entertaining such fantasies, I spent my time, a fat kid with a hernia, constant throat infections, a heart murmur and touch of rheumatic fever, drawing and coloring and modeling clay. When Mom went to the bank she would bring home in her big purse thick packs of white Toledo Trust checking deposit slips. I used the blank backs to make cartoon books filled with bright colors and stories of miraculous rescue or heroic violence. I spent whole days making clay figures—usually Cowboys and Indians, I was no great shakes at originality—and using them to act out adventures I made up as I went along, saying my characters' lines aloud. Dad spoke with pride of my artistic talent. But I caught the doubt in my mother's eyes. I knew she worried that my "art" was only a way of hiding from the world, and that she feared I would turn out like my father, a man too afraid of life to go out into it, hiding behind an unprovable illness, sleeping away the days in a small airless bedroom with blankets tacked over the windows, and prowling the apartment at night like something caged.

I'd be a success at something, I told her, although secretly I felt sure to fail at anything I tried. How could I hope to match my grandfather and my Uncle Frank for courage? What could I hope to do to strike it rich and save our family? And, at another level, I wasn't even sure how hard I was supposed to try. The message I got was mixed. On the one hand we Flanagans were nobodies in a world where being somebody meant that you were corrupt. Our poverty and obscurity were proofs of our virtue. "Look at *her*," my mother would say of someone dressed fancily at Sunday Mass, dismissing the pretender with a sniff. She scorned the man who owned our building, a fellow whose only interests were money and lording it over others. Her goal for me was that I'd hold a steady job—at Champion Spark Plug if need be, though maybe I could get in at Owens-Illinois where my sister Mona worked, or better yet at the Post Office where you didn't get laid off. On the other hand our family played *Monopoly* with a passion, Mom and Dad bet the slots and numbers in hopes of making a killing, and Dad's chatter was filled with envy of those in power. "I'll bet you that you might turn out to be rich and famous," he'd say to me, always when Mom wasn't home, and usually when he wanted me to feel better about some trouble at school or an argument we'd had that he couldn't patch up by giving me a bowl of ice cream, his standard remedy. "No, really, it could happen, Bobby. You just have to have an idea. Like the Parker Brothers." Over the years that became his repeated hope for me: "Maybe someday you'll have an idea."

Back then I never thought of being a writer. Dad had been a writer, briefly: a crime reporter for the old *Newsbee* and, partly due to his flowing Palmer Method handwriting, an executive secretary to The Toledo *Blade* editor. Where had it gotten him? (Of course, where had anything gotten him? He'd been a salesman for a meat company, a used furniture store owner, a bankrupt, a dock worker in a tobacco warehouse, a short order cook, a patient in a veteran's hospital, and finally a recluse. It was not a history to give his son confidence.) And although we were a talky family, we weren't literary. We told jokes, we played word games, Twenty Questions and What's Your Trade, we recited Thomas Moore songs my father had learned from his father and I from him, "Oh believe me if all those endearing young charms," and we admired the newspaper columns of Jim Bishop and the delivery of Don Dunphy doing the Friday night fights. The only reading materials in the apartment were *The Ring* magazine and *Police Gazette*, Dad's paperback copy of Dale Carnegie's *How to Win Friends and Influence People*, and Mom's *Laugh With Leacock*, a hardcover which I think had belonged to her father. How religiously we took Carnegie's American principles of business success. How hard we laughed at the Canadian Leacock's parodies, from which Dad might read aloud some nights when he'd had a few, as in "Gertrude the

Governess" when the romantic Lord Ronald, rebuked by his father, Lord Knotacent, the Earl of Knotacentinum Towers, pronounced Nosham Taws, "flung himself from the room, flung himself upon his horse and rode madly off in all directions." "Oh Laws," my mother would cry, wiping away tears and struggling for breath, "that darn fool!"

I did some reading on my own, mostly *Men at War* and *Classic* comic books. I owned two real books. My aunt Margaret, a schoolteacher, gave me the first one for Christmas when I was nine, *Boru: The Story of an Irish Wolfhound*, and I read it again and again. On my tenth birthday in April, maybe because I'd been begging for a dog despite the rule against pets in the apartment, Dad gave me *Wild Animals of the World*, a large-size dictionary of wildlife with beautiful, realistic illustrations, many in color. I'd never seen anything like it. I just about memorized the book. Dad liked to quiz me on it to impress my uncles. Quagga? "This partly-striped animal believed to have been related both to the zebra and to the wild ass is now extinct." Tapir? "The Tapir has been picturesquely but unscientifically described as a pig that started out to be an elephant and then changed its mind." Seeing me reading and rereading the same two books prompted my sister, Mona Mary, who studied art at Notre Dame Academy, was the proponent of higher culture in our family, and was often put in the role of mother, to lead me to the Dorr Street branch library. There I found books that fed my desire to escape into dreams of power: Jack London's *The Call of the Wild* and *White Fang*, Rudyard Kipling's *The Jungle Book*, Mark Twain's *A Connecticut Yankee in King Arthur's Court*, and, one of my favorites, Henry Gregor Felsen's *Street Rod*. Some years later I picked up the family Bible which I'd never seen anyone open and got lost in Old Testament battles. I would lie on my bed reading Judges and Samuel and Kings. My father kept asking me if everything was all right; behind my back he told my mother he was afraid I'd gone off the deep end.

It wasn't only my Bible reading that worried him. If I wanted to buy a paper route, or to join the Boy Scouts, he immediately sensed danger and predicted disaster. "Now why do you want to start something like that?" he'd complain. "Why can't you just leave well enough alone?" Out of fear, he actively encouraged me to do nothing. Because things were sure to turn out badly, the safest tactic was to keep still. Part of me came to believe that, and often I felt nailed in place. But another part of me resented and resisted inaction. In my late teens, to my father's dismay, the active part of me more and more took over. I sent away for Charles Atlas's Dynamic Tension body building book, and ordered correspondence courses in cartooning and gun repair; I took up the guitar; I won a Saint Genesius medal (the patron saint of actors) for Best Actor in a Catholic Youth Organization drama festival; I did sit-ups until my hernia was declared healed and I could throw away the hated leather truss; I practiced with handgun and rifle and became a crack shot; I thumped the heavy bag and made the light bag dance; I drag-raced "borrowed" cars like a maniac.

Yet the fear was there, all the same. Especially if I let myself think about Uncle Frank.

Francis L. Delora was six feet four inches tall and weighed over two hundred and fifty pounds. Retired from the force after forty-six years of service, 1908 to 1954, he still was a formidable figure. In fact, he was my image of God. He had a huge lion-like head with silver hair brushed straight back, a broad leathery red face, and hands that would make two of mine. He wore gold-rimmed glasses, a gold wedding band, and his gold retirement watch. Even in retirement he often packed his service pistol, a 32.20 Colt Police Positive.

The events that follow still confuse me, as they did when they occurred. I can't say for certain what happened; I only know what I think I remember, a memory distorted by pain.

One night when I was sixteen and had just come home from a high school dance, Dad got a phone call from his sister Nora. A great-hearted, fat-billowing woman, who suffered from cataracts and hardening of the arteries, Nora was upset because she "couldn't get Frankie to wake up." Dad began hunting his car keys and fumbling around for a pair of trousers. Mom was due home from work at any minute. I went on ahead, running up to Frank's and Nora's apartment on Lawrence Avenue. When I knocked, Aunt Nora opened the door a crack and said to come in. I pushed on the door but it stuck. Finally I squeezed through, stumbling over Uncle Frank. He lay on his back just inside the door, his neck bent and head propped on the baseboard. Aunt Nora had wedged a pillow behind his head to make him comfortable. She moved off down the hall, saying that she was cooking Frankie a hamburger; he'd feel better if he'd only eat a little something. I could smell whiskey on him. I called to him and pulled on his wrists to get him to sit up. He was so heavy I couldn't move him. His big hands felt cold. Greasy smoke and the smell of charred meat floated in from the kitchen. My fingers touched the back of his head. It felt pulpy, like a squashed melon. My hand came away covered with blood.

Dad and Mom showed up, and the police. Frank had been in a fight with his brother Hank in a bar. Hank was every bit as big as Frank and they were tearing up the place. It took a half-dozen officers to get them calmed down. Then, as a courtesy to Frank, a squad car had run the Delora boys home. Both brothers were banged up, the Polish police captain told us, but Frank must have been hurt a lot worse than he looked. It was a terrible thing, though it'd be best to call it a fall, an accident. We wouldn't want to start something that could get the man's own brother charged with manslaughter, would we?

At home Mom and Dad phoned Hank, who said that the cruiser had dropped him off first, and that Frank had been okay then, except for a couple of scratches. After the call, we sat at the kitchen table, Dad saying how it had to be the cops. Everybody knew the way Frank bullied patrolmen, and how hard he was to handle when he was on the sauce. One of those rookies, Dad said, had used a sap harder than he'd meant to, that was the truth of it, then they panicked and dumped the body and got the hell out of there, the lousy lying murdering bums. There wasn't one damn thing we could do about it, either.

For some time after I lay awake nights imagining myself tracking down the rookie to ambush him with Frank's own pistol. In school I'd daydream about getting the Polish Captain too, making sure he recognized me before I let him have it. But finally I just tried not to think about Uncle Frank. Whenever I let myself dwell on it—so much power so easily destroyed!—I'd feel my father's paralysis creeping over me.

After high school I went to work. I worked as night watchman at the Family Fair department store at Bancroft and Auburn, 10 P.M. to 7 A.M., Monday through Saturday. I liked the job because I was left alone and got to carry a gun; it was a .38 American Bulldog, one of Uncle Frank's revolvers that Dad had handed on to me when Aunt Nora died. I worked as janitor at the truck terminals out on Tractor Road, day laborer for a landscaper, and utility man at Republic Steel. I worked as dishwasher at the Waffle Inn downtown by the Town Hall Burlesque. The strippers would come in for coffee and donuts in the afternoon, sexy, scary women with hard faces and harsh, smokey laughs. They called me Kid and said why didn't I drop in and catch their act. I wanted to, but was way too leery of them. After washing dishes, having taken up boxing as a manly alternative to the neighborhood streetfights I dreaded, I'd walk to the Y and work out. I'd lost enough weight in training to be taken for a middleweight, a coach told me I had a snappy jab, and one wonderful afternoon a sparring partner went down after bouncing off the ropes into my defensive, stiff-armed right. I thought maybe I'd found my calling, and talked of going into the Golden Gloves. This despite the fact that I had no power, possessed a suspect jaw and small breakable hands, had worn glasses since the fourth grade and saw my opponent in the ring as a moving blur. Getting cold-cocked a couple of times cleared my head of that fiction.

When I'd quit a handful of dead-end jobs in the year since graduating from high school, and when I had no idea what I was doing or where I was going, and was scared that I was proving to be just like my father, I had a beer with a high school buddy in a bar on Toledo's east side. He told me that first thing in the morning he was going downtown to join the Marines. I said, "Pick me up."

It seemed to me that I was doing something to show how different I was from my father, the ex-Marine, by joining the Marines. Why I thought that then I don't know now.

At Parris Island I got to talk to guys who'd gone to college (because my friend and I had joined the reserves) and I noticed that they didn't seem that much smarter than I was. As soon as I finished my six months active duty, I enrolled at the University of Toledo, the only college I'd heard of except for Notre Dame, home of the Fighting Irish, whose fight song we'd copied for ours at Central Catholic High.

It was then that I began reading seriously. The works which most influenced me at that time were the stories of Frank O'Connor, so natural sounding I might have been hearing them told around our kitchen table, the plays of Eugene O'Neill, which seemed to spring right out of the Old Testament, and James T. Farrell's Studs Lonigan novels: *Young Lonigan, The Young Manhood of Studs Lonigan,* and *Judgment Day.* In Farrell's work I recognized the characters I saw around me every day and it struck me that I might write about the people in my own life, even in Toledo.

At twenty-one, I started writing some poems and stories of my own. I didn't write many because I was going to college days and working nights and spending as much time as I could with a great girl I'd found, someone who was good-looking and spunky and took me seriously.

I read Jack London's *Martin Eden* which excited me so much I decided to make my living as a writer. I knocked out a dozen stories and rushed them off to men's magazines and they bounced right back. The stories for the most part were accounts of things I'd seen, like a guy in a diner smacking somebody with one of those heavy glass sugar dispensers. I'd never thought of using something like that as a weapon and I wrote a story about an unarmed man trapped in a diner by a punk with a knife. I got John Brick, a visiting instructor and published novelist, to read it and he said "Okay, but the only thing that happens in this is that one fellow hits the other with a sugar jar." I said, "Right! Like it?" He suggested that I sign up for his fiction writing course the next semester which, thank my lucky stars, I did.

Also in those first bursts of work I wrote a play and got the chance to put it on at the university. Entitled "The Discontent," it was imitation O'Neill with some Ibsen tossed in and presented as the symbol of a family's despair an heirloom music box that had been wound so tight that it finally snapped. I directed the production as well as played the lead role of the father, a failed artist. I also helped to build the set, a kitchen, and hauled in a real sink as a final, convincing touch. The play, which dealt with art, history, war, love, courage, the family, and alcoholism, ran a bit long for one act. The action consisted mainly of declamatory speeches which sounded like blank verse and gave the work, I thought, a certain tragic dimension. After the performance, the doyenne of the theatre department stopped by to say, "Well, Flanagan, you put in everything *and* the kitchen sink."

My first published work, a poem entitled "The Rift," was inspired by a break-up with my new girlfriend. I'd written it in the middle of the night in a Bancroft Avenue laundromat, conditions which struck me as romantic and artistic. That the poem depended on a metaphor based on cows, animals I knew nothing about, didn't matter. My girl and I got back together and the poem was published in *The Small Pond*, a little magazine in the east. Such publication, I thought, confirmed my calling.

In my junior year of college, at twenty-two, I quit breaking up with my girl and married her. Kathleen Rose Borer was from Ottawa, Ohio where she'd grown up poor in a family with a troubled, troublesome father, and had come to Toledo to take her nurse's training at St. Vincent's Hospital on Cherry Street. At the time she had it in mind to become an Air Force nurse and see the world. I'd met her on a blind date arranged by some friends who'd gone to Central Catholic with me and were in training with Katy at Saint V's. Maybe they thought I needed a nurse to care for me; in those days, and for too long after, I acted as though I did. I'd ride around nights with two other aspiring writers from Irish families, talking literature and drinking and looking for trouble; one night we took a tiny Fiat cross-country over the Ottawa Park golf course as I fired my .38 at trees. Whatever the nursing students' motives, they did me a great favor. I've never known a person of deeper patience or more genuine independence of spirit than Katy; her understanding of people has helped give some depth to my fiction's characters.

Two years after our wedding, expecting our first child in three months, we left Toledo for Chicago, the literary turf of James T. Farrell and Nelson Algren and Richard Wright and Theodore Dreiser, writers I regarded as gods, and of a fairly new guy I thought showed promise, Saul Bellow. Why would *anyone* ever go to New York when there was Chicago? I could not believe my good luck. I had won a full fellowship in Theology and Literature because George Guthrie, my philosophy professor at Toledo, had taken me aside one day after class to inquire about my future. I thought I'd stay on at the city streets department, I told him, where I'd been working summers, driving weed mowers and trucks, and would write at night. It shouldn't be long before I made some money; I'd already had a poem published. He told me that I ought to consider graduate school. I said okay, and applied to the one place he mentioned, his alma mater, the University of Chicago.

When Katy and I drove out of town in a U-Haul truck, we passed a billboard proclaiming the Glass Center of the World. Despite the promise of our future, I felt the truth in that phrase. It was what I had learned growing up. Everything about you was breakable.

It's that knowledge which informs my fiction.

Our Photographers

Charles Cassady, Jr. lives in Lakewood, Ohio, and captures images of Northern Ohio in his photography.

Robert Fox is a writer, blues musician and occasional photographer now living in Columbus. He is also the literature coordinator of the Ohio Arts Council. His essay, "The Farm Not Taken," is included here.

Dennis Horan is a native of Sandusky, Ohio and a graduate of Ohio University and Bowling Green State University. He is the director of Firelands College Knowledge Network. His nature photos have graced the pages of many publications.

Becky Linhardt lives in Columbus and graduated from the University of Cincinnati. She is active in the arts as an exhibition coordinator for the Reynoldsburg Arts Commission and Director of Gallery Programs at Capital University Law Library. Her images have appeared in *Airfare*, Columbus Symphony Orchestra Calendars, and PrinTech 1992 Ohio Artists' Calendar. She is also an active nonfiction writer whose writing has appeared in *The Columbus Dispatch*, *Columbus Art*, and *Columbus Homes and Lifestyles*.

Stephen J. Ostrander lives in Columbus where he is active in the arts of writing and photography. His essay, "On Names, Places, and Times" opens this collection. He is a former newspaper editor who now works at writing field guides to the nature preserves in Ohio and Pennsylvania. His work reveals his faith in knowing a place through mapping it out in images.

Our Editors

John Moor and **Larry Smith** teach writing at Firelands College of Bowling Green State University in Huron, Ohio. Both are natives of Ohio.

John Moor is a graduate of Bowling Green State University with a double emphasis in English and journalism. His writings on religion and on local affairs have been published.

Larry Smith's essay, "The Company of Widows," appears in this issue. He is director of the Firelands Writing Center and co-editor of *The Heartlands Today*. His sixth book of poetry, *Steel Valley: Postcards and Letters*, appeared last year from Pig Iron Press of Youngstown. He also directs Bottom Dog Press.

Special Contributors

Rita Dove is a native of Akron, Ohio, and our country's Poet Laureate. Her books of poetry include *The Yellow House on the Corner* (1980), *Museum* (1983), *Thomas and Beulah* (1986), winner of the Pulitzer Prize, *Grace Notes* (1989), and *Selected Poems* (1993). Her fiction includes the story collection *Fifth Sunday* (1985) and the novel *Through the Ivory Gate* (1992).

Scott Russell Sanders grew up in Ohio in the town of Wayland, just outside the Ravenna arsenal. He is an active editor, fiction writer, and essayist. His most recent books include *A Paradise of Bombs* (1987), *Secrets of the Universe: Scenes from the Journey Home* (1991), and *Staying Put: Making a Home in a Restless World* (1993).

Bottom Dog Press books are published in Ohio.
For a complete listing, write to:
Bottom Dog Press
c/o Firelands College
Huron, Ohio 44839